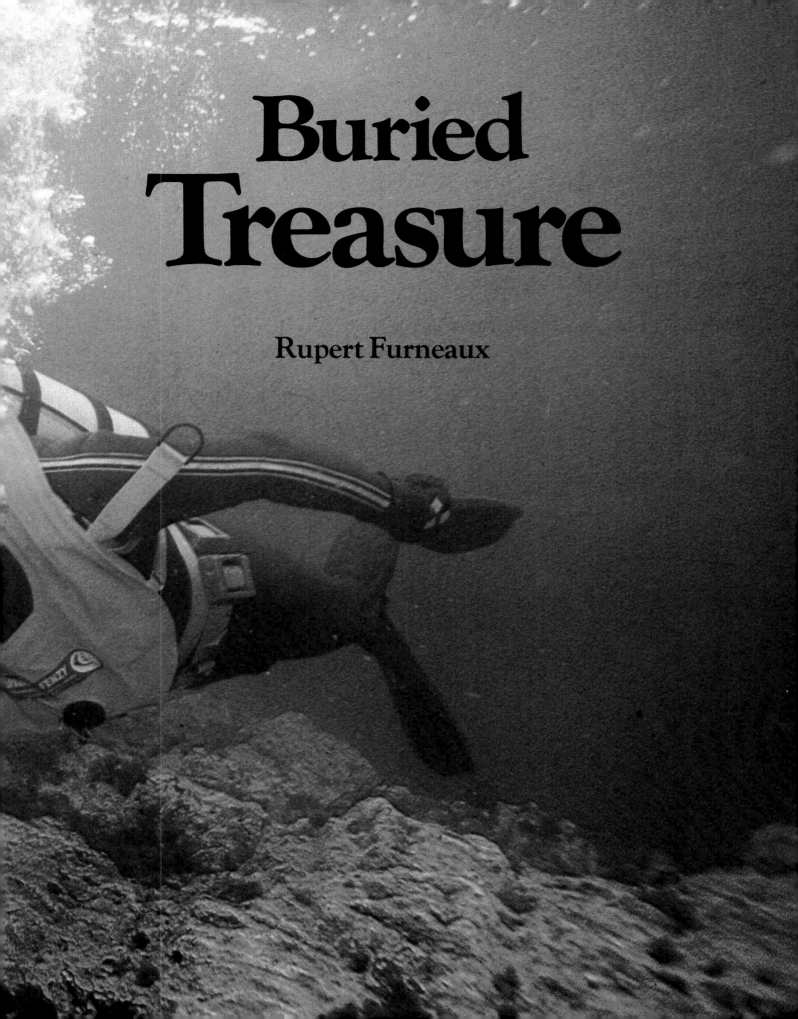

Buried
Treasure

Rupert Furneaux

First published in 1978 by
Macdonald Educational Ltd
Holywell House
Worship Street
London EC2A 2EN

ISBN 0 356 06108 6

Printed and bound by
Purnell & Sons Ltd
Paulton
Avon
England

Illustration credits

Key to the position of illustrations: (T) top; (C) centre; (B) bottom; and combinations, for example: (TR) top right; (CL) centre left.

Artists
Max Ansell/Temple Art: 6–7, 11, 14, 34–5, 46, 49, 55
C. L. Doughty/Temple Art: 15
M. Whittlesea/Temple Art: 31
Jeff Burn/Temple Art: 52–3 (T)
Donald Harley/B. L. Kearley Ltd: 12–13
Tony Payne: 18–19
Peter North: 10, 24–5, 28, 36–7
Ralph Stobart: 29, 38–9
Jenny Thorne/Linda Rogers Associates: 32, 45
Michael McGuinness: 48–9
Hayward Art Group: cover illustration and maps

Photographs
John M. Allegro: 14 (CL)
Joan Allen Electronics: 59 (B)
Peter Clayton: 8–9
Daily Telegraph Colour Library: 34 (T), 35 (T), 36 (T), 37 (T), 46 TL), 47 (BR)
Mary Evans Picture Library: 50 (B)
Ruper Furneaux: 54 (T), 54 (C)
Griffith Institute: 10–11 (B), 11 (BR)
Robert Harding: 11 (TL)
Historical Society of Philadelphia: 55 (T)
Miss Mercie Lack and Henry Bailey King: 18 (T)
Mansell Collection: 27 (B), 30 (BL), 43 (T), 43 (BL)
National Maritime Museum: 23 (BR), 32–3 (B), 35 (BC), 40–41, 42 (BL)
National Portrait Gallery: 29 (CL)
Public Record Office: 20–21
Radio Times Hulton Picture Library: 42 (CB), 42 (BR), 43 (BR), 44 (BR), 45 (CL), 50 (TL), 58
Oronoz: 27 (T), 49 (BL)
Seaphot: 4–5, 59 (TL), 59 (TR)
Photri: 53 (BR)
Ronald Sheridan: 15 (TR), 17
Society of Apothecaries: 22–3 (T)
Sorima: 39 (BR)
Robert Stenuit: 24 (BL), 25 (BL)
By kind permission of the Marquess of Tavistock and the Trustees of the Bedford Estates: 23 (CL)

Contents

History Comes Alive

Tutankhamun's tomb

'Yes, wonderful things!' Howard Carter was replying to Lord Carnarvon's question 'Can you see anything?' The archaeologist and his financial backer were standing at the door of a tomb they had found in the Valley of the Kings, at Luxor in Egypt. The valley was the burial place of thirty pharaohs.

Contrary to the opinion of many archaeologists who had searched the valley, Carter was convinced that one more tomb remained to be found – that of the boy king Tutankhamun who had reigned about 1350 B.C. Now, in 1922, Carter stood at the outer door of the tomb, approached by a flight of steps. Had the tomb been looted by tomb robbers as all the others had been?

Removal of the door showed an anteroom filled with the goods the pharaohs took with them to the grave to ensure their well-being in the afterlife. Yet another door gave entrance to the tomb chamber itself. Three golden shrines, one within another, almost filled the chamber.

Inside these shrines was yet another wonder, the sarcophagus, or coffin, itself surmounted by Tutankhamun's effigy made of solid gold. Beneath the massive lid Carter found three golden caskets, one within another, the last containing the mummified body of the king. It was intact, just as it had been laid to rest over three thousand years ago. On its breast lay a posy of flowers, perhaps the last offering of the widowed queen.

It took Howard Carter and his helpers years to clear the tomb. Each article had to be preserved and wrapped before being taken to the Cairo Museum. But the pharaoh's body was not removed. It remains in the tomb, still surmounted by his golden effigy.

Tutankhamun's wealth, the greatest of all archaeological treasures, is priceless. Carter's discovery of the tomb thrilled the world in the 1920s. Then a shadow fell across those involved in the discovery.

Within six weeks of the tomb's opening, Lord Carnarvon sickened and died, following a mosquito bite. There were many people who believed that the opening of the tomb was a sacrilege which would call down on the heads of the archaeologists the wrath of the ancient gods, and the revenge of the dead pharaoh's spirit. Within the next ten years twenty people who had been connected with the tomb's opening died, apparently mysteriously. Were they also victims of the Curse of the Pharaohs? But Howard Carter lived until 1939, dying at the age of sixty-six.

Leading Egyptologists who have spent their lives revealing Egypt's past, dismiss the Curse as pure fantasy. The most famous Egyptologist of all, Sir Flinders Petrie, died aged eighty-nine. Nor would the pharaohs have laid such curses. They would have known that curses were futile. To preserve their bodies, the pharaohs built and excavated massive fortresses, but to no avail. All except Tutankhamun were torn from their resting places by robbers in their search for gold.

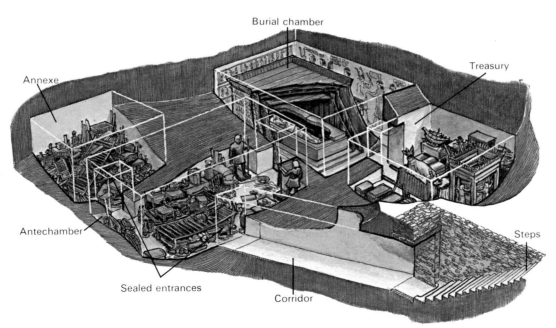

Burial chamber

Treasury

Annexe

Antechamber

Sealed entrances

Corridor

Steps

▲ A flight of sixteen steps led down to the entrance of Tutankhamun's tomb. The sealed doorway was removed and beyond it lay a sloping corridor filled with rubble. Another sealed doorway gave on to the antechamber and the other three rooms which contained Tutankhamun's treasure. Although there was evidence that robbers had visited the tomb, most of the treasure was intact. It took Carter and his team ten years to clear the tomb and transport the treasure to the Cairo Museum.

The pharaoh's treasure

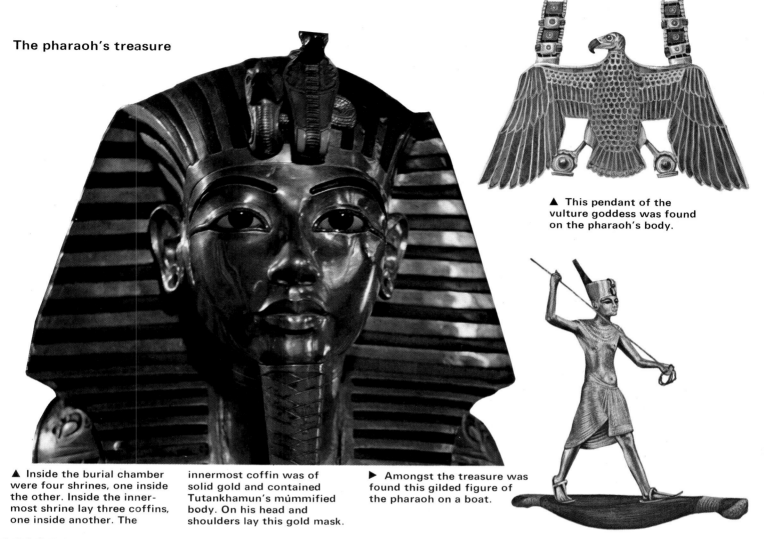

▲ This pendant of the vulture goddess was found on the pharaoh's body.

▲ Inside the burial chamber were four shrines, one inside the other. Inside the innermost shrine lay three coffins, one inside another. The innermost coffin was of solid gold and contained Tutankhamun's mummified body. On his head and shoulders lay this gold mask.

▶ Amongst the treasure was found this gilded figure of the pharaoh on a boat.

◀ The interior of the antechamber as Carter first saw it. The room was full of precious objects and furniture including this gilded couch.

▲ Howard Carter and Lord Carnarvon at the entrance to the fourth shrine. Inside the shrine lay the coffins and the mummified body of the pharaoh.

The Dorak treasure

During the 1950s James Mellaart was a promising young archaeologist who had taken part in several digs in Turkey. In the summer of 1958 he was travelling by train to the town of Izmir on the coast of Turkey.

Mellaart noticed that the woman was wearing a solid gold bracelet which excited his interest at once. He was convinced that it was very old, perhaps even prehistoric, and therefore very valuable. He started talking to the woman and soon the conversation turned to the bracelet.

The woman told Mellaart that the bracelet was part

Towards evening, the train began to get full and Mellaart moved to another compartment. Shortly afterwards a young woman came in and sat opposite him.

of a collection of old pieces and invited him to her house in Izmir to see them. Apparently this treasure had recently been found in an old tomb near Dorak.

The woman gave her name as Anna Papastrati and took Mellaart to number 217 Kazim Dirik Street, which she said belonged to her father. Mellaart stayed at the house making detailed notes and drawings of the treasure. The objects included the figures of a goddess and her handmaidens decorated with gold and silver ornaments as well as precious jewellery, swords and daggers. To Mellaart's experienced eyes it looked as though the treasure was a major archaeological find, relics of the ancient Yortan people who had lived close to Troy.

Mellaart notified the British Institute of Archaeology and the Turkish authorities of his discovery, and the following year published an article on the treasure in the *Illustrated London News*. The magazine headed the article 'The Royal Treasure of Dorak' and described it as the 'first and exclusive report of a clandestine excavation'. In the meantime Mellaart continued his archaeological work in Turkey.

The publication of Mellaart's article caused an outcry in Turkey. One newspaper ran a campaign against Mellaart suggesting that he had found the treasure and smuggled it out of Turkey himself.

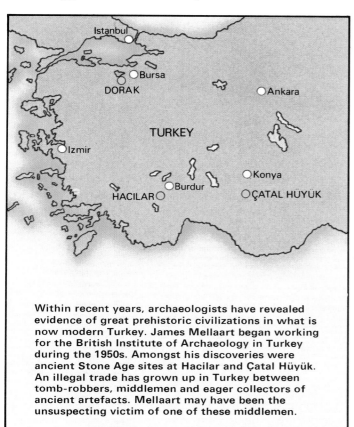

Within recent years, archaeologists have revealed evidence of great prehistoric civilizations in what is now modern Turkey. James Mellaart began working for the British Institute of Archaeology in Turkey during the 1950s. Amongst his discoveries were ancient Stone Age sites at Hacilar and Çatal Hüyük. An illegal trade has grown up in Turkey between tomb-robbers, middlemen and eager collectors of ancient artefacts. Mellaart may have been the unsuspecting victim of one of these middlemen.

Investigations were made to check Mellaart's claims, and at this point the story becomes very strange. Anna Papastrati could not be traced, nor could the house to which she had taken Mellaart. However, at Dorak there was no sign of recent excavations. Mellaart was unable to renew his permit to dig in Turkey while the Dorak story was being investigated. But eventually nothing could be proved against him.

The treasure had disappeared along with Anna Papastrati. Had it ever existed? It seems so, for Mellaart could hardly have imagined such unique articles. An archaeologist of his reputation would have no need to invent a non-existent find in order to further his career.

Throughout the world museum curators and private collectors compete with one another to buy rare antiquities for their collections. In many cases the negotiations are conducted through middlemen, international dealers who do not reveal the seller's identity. Often this is because the antiquity has been illegally smuggled out of its country of origin.

Mellaart, it seems, had been used to publish pictures of the Dorak treasure to establish its authenticity before it was disposed of on the black market. Anna Papastrati must have been planted on the train to catch the eye of the reputable archaeologist.

The treasure of Dorak may now lie in some museum vault or in the safe of a wealthy private collector. One thing seems certain. The treasure cannot be shown publicly for some time, as it would be recognized as smuggled goods, the property of the Turkish government.

The smuggling of ancient relics out of Turkey is nothing new. Many rare objects have suffered that fate despite the vigilance of the Turkish Department of Antiquities. It is impossible to guard all the ancient sites in Turkey. While Mellaart was excavating the prehistoric site at Hacilar, the cemetery was looted for ancient objects by people without official permission to dig. In the bazaars of Turkish cities dealers will offer rare antiquities to tourists and dealers who have the money to pay for them.

The Copper Scroll: clues to an ancient mystery

▲ When found, the Copper Scroll had fallen into two pieces. The copper was brittle and oxidised, and it was impossible to unroll it.

▼ The Scroll was sent to the Manchester College of Technology where a special machine was built to cut it into sections.

In A.D. 70 the Romans besieged and destroyed Jerusalem, the holy city of the Jews who had risen in revolt. The Romans looted the city and took to Rome the sacred vessels of the Temple, the seven-branched candlestick and the table of shewbread, which were displayed in General Titus's Triumph.

The Jews also kept great private wealth at the Temple bank in Jerusalem. Did the Roman soldiers get it all, or did the Jews, fearing the fall of the city, conceal some of it? That appears to be the message of the Copper Scroll.

The discovery in 1947 of a number of ancient scrolls within caves in the cliffs overlooking the Dead Sea excited scholars because they threw new light on Biblical history. One of these scrolls was different from the others. Its letters had been hammered out on copper, presumably because its message was particularly important and required permanent survival.

The message of the Copper Scroll has been deciphered by John Allegro, a Biblical scholar and lecturer in Semitic languages. The Scroll, he believes, provides clues for the discovery of an immense treasure concealed by the Zealots, a group of Jewish nationalists, before the fall of Jerusalem.

No Roman, had he discovered the Scroll, could have unravelled its clues. The Zealot scribe cloaked his various clues to the hiding places in language which could be understood only by people who remembered ancient place names and understood obscure Biblical references.

The Scroll indicates treasure sites in three main areas: in the hills above the Dead Sea, near the city of Jericho, and in and around Jerusalem. One such clue reads:

'In the fortress which is in the Vale of Acor, forty cubits under the steps entering to the east: a money chest and its contents, of a weight of seventeen talents.

The treasure sites mentioned in the Copper Scroll come into three main areas: Dead Sea sites (including Qumran), sites around Jericho, and the city of Jerusalem. John Allegro's theory suggests that the Zealots were the only group who had control over these sites during the war with the Romans. The Copper Scroll may be an inventory of the treasure which the Zealots amassed to finance the war. As far as we know, the safely-hidden treasure has never been recovered.

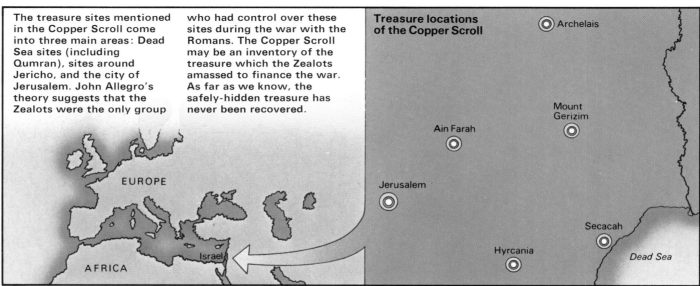

EUROPE

AFRICA

Israel

Treasure locations of the Copper Scroll

Archelais

Mount Gerizim

Ain Farah

Jerusalem

Secacah

Hyrcania

Dead Sea

'In the sepulchral monument, in the third course of stones : eight bars of gold.'

The term 'talent', Allegro believes, denoted a silver coin weighing twelve modern ounces. To find these coins Allegro needed to locate the Vale of Acor. No such name now exists. It may be the deep gorge running to the west of the Dead Sea and about six miles from Jerusalem, which needed to be protected by a fortress. One was built there by the Jewish king Hyrcanus (135–104 B.C.) and its ruins still exist.

Allegro searched these ruins, known as the Hyrcania, in 1960. No steps 'entering from the east' could be traced but nearby he identified the 'sepulchral monument' as the tomb of Herod Antipater. Fearing to destroy archaeological evidence, Allegro did not excavate deeply. He did, however, find a number of silver coins beneath the sect's monastery, where another clue pointed to a deposit.

The Zealots hid the bulk of the treasure in and around Jerusalem. The Israelis are now carrying out extensive excavations within the Old City of Jerusalem. Maybe they will come across some of the hiding places of the treasure concealed by the Zealots. The clues provided by the Copper Scroll may guide them.

▲ A section of the relief on the Arch of Titus in Rome. It shows soldiers carrying the Temple treasures including the seven-branched candlestick.

▼ The Romans attacking the Temple in A.D. 70. The Temple treasures were taken to Rome, but did the Jews hide other treasure outside the city ?

The Panagyurishte treasure

Workmen were digging for clay at Panagyurishte, between the towns of Sofia and Plovdiv, in Bulgaria in 1949. They unearthed eight drinking vessels and a broad, flat vessel, all made of solid gold and weighing 6 kilos (13 lbs). This treasure of immense value is now exhibited in the museum at Plovdiv.

Following its discovery, the treasure was examined by Bulgarian archaeologists. Who had made these beautiful vases and cups, and where? How old were they? Dr Ivan Venedikov, curator of the National Museum, searched for clues.

The concealment of the objects in a shallow hole far from any inhabited spot suggested they had been hastily buried, possibly by someone fleeing from danger. The region surrounding Panagyurishte had been part of Thrace, a land lying to the north of ancient Greece. It had been conquered by the Celts around 350 B.C.

It took little imagination to suggest that this rich hoard had belonged to some Thracian noble. Pursued by the Celts, he had concealed his wealth before his capture and death. Where had he bought these beautiful objects? The obvious answer seemed to be Greece, where craftsmen were famous for their exquisite work in gold and silver. But Venedikov noticed facts which disproved their Greek origin. How he unravelled the clues is a remarkable story of archaeological detection.

The treasure consists of eight drinking vessels and a phiale, or broad, flat vessel, such as were used at banquets. Seven of the drinking vessels are shaped in the form of animals and women's heads. They portray the gods and heroes of Greek mythology, such as Aphrodite and Theseus. The eighth drinking vessel has two handles in the form of centaurs and is engraved with five warriors. The names of the Greek gods were inscribed on the vessels in the form which had been adopted in the Greek cities of Asia Minor after the death of Alexander the Great in 323 B.C.

The vessels were below the standard of Greek workmanship and Venedikov noticed a foreign influence. He suspected they had been made close to ancient Greece by people who had a more oriental form of art, probably Persian.

The weights engraved on the vessels by their makers proved their origin. The weights were given in two forms, by the Greek method, and according to the Persian system. Only one city in Asia Minor (modern Turkey) had used both measures. That was Lampsacus, the modern Lâpseki. Following Alexander's conquests, the Greek system had replaced the Persian one and the makers of the vases had added the Greek measures.

Venedikov assumed that the buyer had bought his treasures one by one, converting his wealth into easily movable objects. He must have guessed that dangerous times lay ahead following Alexander's death and the break up of his empire. Events proved him right. When Thrace, his homeland, was invaded by the Celts he tried to escape, carrying his wealth. But despite the prudence he had shown, he obviously left it too late and had to abandon the treasure during his flight.

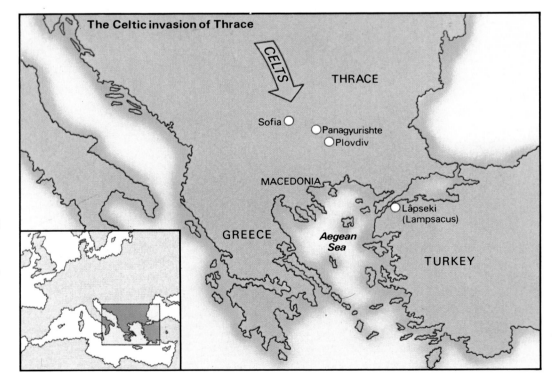

▶ About the year 350 B.C. the country of Thrace (modern Bulgaria) was invaded from the north by fierce Celts. It is thought that a rich Thracian nobleman, fearing for his life and property, sought to escape. He carried with him his wealth, which he had converted into easily-transportable gold vessels. Unable to shake off his pursuers, he hastily buried his hoard. Whether he made his escape or not, we do not know for he did not return to recover the vessels. They were discovered in 1949, and archaeologists have since traced the origin of the vessels. They were made in Lampsacus, now the modern town of Lâpseki, in Turkey.

The Celtic invasion of Thrace

CELTS

THRACE

Sofia ○
○ Panagyurishte
○ Plovdiv

MACEDONIA

GREECE   Aegean Sea

○ Lâpseki (Lampsacus)

TURKEY

▲ The hoard included a gold drinking vessel or rhyton, in the form of a stag's head. The liquid was drunk through the opening in the stag's mouth. The neck of the vessel shows the figures of Greek gods.

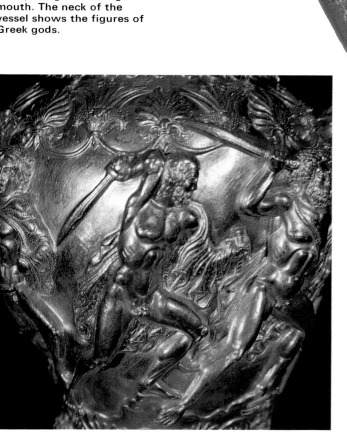

◄ Part of the amphora-rhyton. The scene on the side shows five warriors wearing flowing cloaks. They are wielding swords, and one is playing a trumpet. The handles of the vessel are in the form of centaurs, creatures from Greek mythology. There are two openings at the top of the vessel which made it possible for two people to drink from it at the same time.

▲ The phiale measures 25 cm in diameter. The decorations were made individually and then soldered onto the vessel with silver. There are three bands of human heads in gold and a band of acorns near the centre. The vessel's weight is engraved according to the Greek and Persian systems.

Sutton Hoo: a ship buried on land

The mounds at the end of her garden at Sutton Hoo in Suffolk excited Mrs Pretty's curiosity. There were eleven of them on the edge of the cliff overlooking the river Deben. An archaeologist from Norwich Museum told her they were ancient burial mounds made probably by the Anglo-Saxons who had invaded England in the seventh century.

Starting work in May 1939, a team from the British Museum excavated the mounds. Beginning at the largest mound which was 2.7 metres high, 30 metres long and 23 metres wide (9 by 100 by 75 feet), they dug a trench 1.8 metres (6 feet) long. As they worked, their spades turned up clumps of corroded nails – 'clench' nails as they are called from their shape. These indicated a ship burial, the Saxon custom of burying a chief or king.

Careful removal of the earth showed the outlines of a vessel. The shape of the vessel had been retained in the sandy soil long after its wood had decayed. Further digging at Sutton Hoo disclosed the impression of a ship 27 metres long and 4 metres wide (89 by 14 feet). It had been a great open row boat propelled by fourteen oarsmen. It had been carried up from the river, an immense task which had been clearly warranted by the importance of the occasion.

Amidship, the archaeologists found the burial chamber. It contained beautiful and costly objects – the grave goods of a king. But there was no skeleton.

The absence of human remains was intriguing. Several explanations have been put forward. The Saxon king may have been killed in war at a place too distant for his body to be brought home for burial. His subjects had built the mound to contain his ship in his memory. Or they had created a pagan shrine because he had been converted to Christianity and buried in hallowed ground, and they wished to honour the ancient custom. The Saxons were converted to Christianity about A.D. 700.

▲ Archaeologists digging at Sutton Hoo. They found the impression in the earth of a Saxon ship. Its timbers had decayed, leaving none of the woodwork. The iron rivets had survived and lay in their original positions. Archaeologists made a plaster cast of the ship's impression and from this made a fibre-glass reconstruction of the ship.

▼ The Sutton Hoo ship had been clinker-built with overlapping wooden boards. It is thought that the ship was propelled by oars, but it may have had a mast and sail.

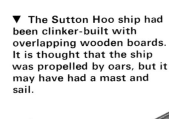

▲ Some of the 37 gold coins which were found in a purse with the treasure. The coins were all made on the Continent.

18

Treasures of a Saxon king

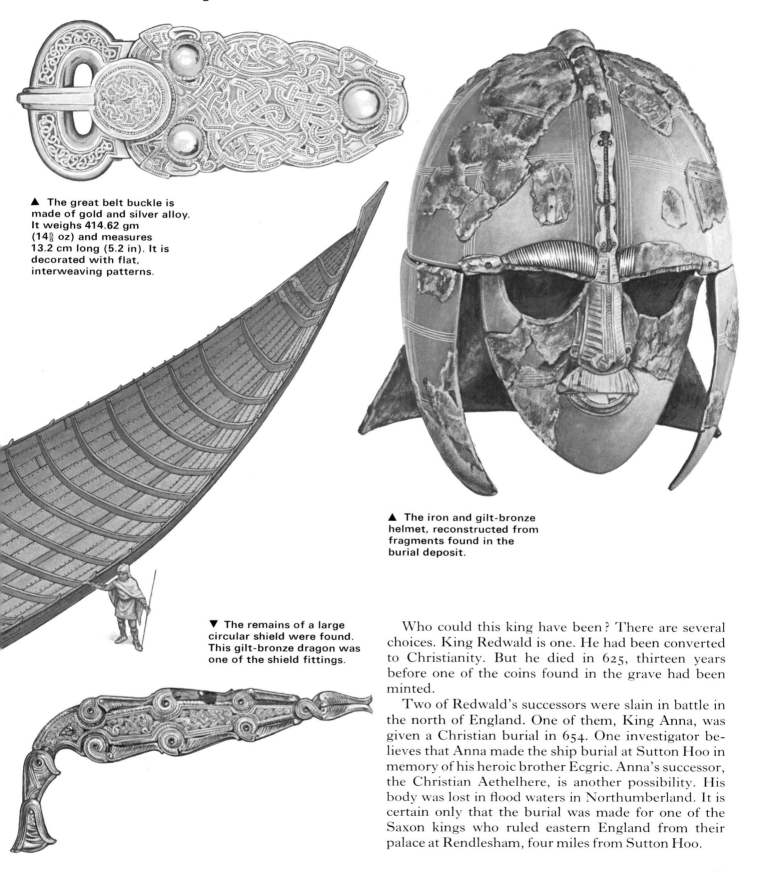

▲ The great belt buckle is made of gold and silver alloy. It weighs 414.62 gm (14⅝ oz) and measures 13.2 cm long (5.2 in). It is decorated with flat, interweaving patterns.

▲ The iron and gilt-bronze helmet, reconstructed from fragments found in the burial deposit.

▼ The remains of a large circular shield were found. This gilt-bronze dragon was one of the shield fittings.

Who could this king have been? There are several choices. King Redwald is one. He had been converted to Christianity. But he died in 625, thirteen years before one of the coins found in the grave had been minted.

Two of Redwald's successors were slain in battle in the north of England. One of them, King Anna, was given a Christian burial in 654. One investigator believes that Anna made the ship burial at Sutton Hoo in memory of his heroic brother Ecgric. Anna's successor, the Christian Aethelhere, is another possibility. His body was lost in flood waters in Northumberland. It is certain only that the burial was made for one of the Saxon kings who ruled eastern England from their palace at Rendlesham, four miles from Sutton Hoo.

Treasure from the Sea

Disaster at sea: the Armada

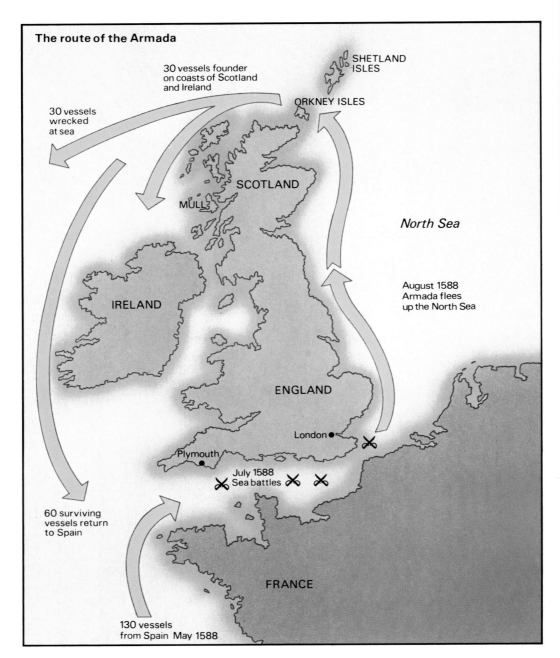

The route of the Armada

30 vessels founder on coasts of Scotland and Ireland

SHETLAND ISLES

30 vessels wrecked at sea

ORKNEY ISLES

SCOTLAND

MULL

North Sea

IRELAND

August 1588 Armada flees up the North Sea

ENGLAND

London

Plymouth

July 1588 Sea battles

60 surviving vessels return to Spain

FRANCE

130 vessels from Spain May 1588

▲ Darting out from the Channel ports, the English 'sea dogs' harried the Armada. The Spanish ships suffered heavy damage, but no English ships were lost.

◄ The Armada sailed up the English Channel. After battles with the English ships, the Spanish fleet fled up the North Sea. Ten of their ships had been lost in battle, and another sixty were wrecked before the remains of the Armada found their way back to Spain.

The mighty Armada, the greatest fleet ever assembled, sailed majestically up the English Channel. Keeping out of range of the heavy Spanish cannon, the nimble English vessels inflicted severe damage. They fired three cannon balls to the Spaniards' one, and put them to flight.

Their hulls leaking, their sails hanging in shreds, their anchors gone, the surviving vessels of the 'invincible' Armada fled up the North Sea. Their captains hoped to sail round Scotland and get their stricken ships home to Spain.

Rounding Scotland the top-heavy, unwieldy galleons met the full force of the Atlantic gales. Autumn storms forced them on to the jagged coasts of Scotland and Ireland. Thirty vessels were wrecked. Another thirty foundered at sea. Sixty limped home to Spain, their crews diseased and starving.

The Armada carried 220,000 golden ducats worth nearly £1,500,000 by today's value. That was the royal treasure to pay the soldiers and sailors, and the cost of invading England. Many of the officers and aristocratic volunteers had also brought their personal fortunes, expecting to acquire English estates. Thus in all the Armada may have carried over £8,500,000. None of it got back to Spain. A large part of that huge treasure may still lie amongst the rocks where the ships were wrecked. The invention of skindiving gear has made its recovery possible, and even profitable.

◄ Queen Elizabeth I incurred the wrath of the Spanish King by aiding Dutch Protestants in their war against Spain. The Queen also encouraged the plunder of Spanish ships by men such as Drake and Hawkins.

▼ King Philip II of Spain embarked upon the invasion of England against the advice of his admirals. This was doomed to failure because there were no ports on the French coast where his ships could take haven for repairs.

There is no doubt of the location of one wreck. It is believed that the galleon which sank in Tobermory Bay on the Scottish island of Mull is the *Florencia*. This vessel is reputed to have carried one of the King of Spain's war chests. Spanish records state that the *Florencia* carried 'thirty millions of cash' stored beneath the gun room. A strong clue points to the wreck being the *Florencia*. The ship was commanded by the Portuguese Don Pereira, and a plate bearing his family crest has been dredged up from the bay. A team of Royal Navy divers located the wreck in 1954. The Duke of Argyll, the owner of the wreck, believes that the treasure can be salvaged despite the fact that it lies beneath thirty feet of mud.

An Armada ship recovered

Don Alonzo de Leiva commanded a squadron of Armada vessels, one of which was a galleas, the *Girona*. A galleas was a ship propelled by both oars and sails. When his own ship and two other vessels were wrecked on the Irish coast, Don de Leiva transferred the 1,300 survivors and their gold and silver to the *Girona*. He set off, hoping to reach Scotland in order to repair his one remaining vessel. Sailing up the Irish coast, the *Girona* also sank. But where?

The general area was not in doubt, for the local chieftain, James MacDonald of Dunluce Castle, salvaged cannon and money from the wreck. The ruins of Dunluce Castle still exist in County Antrim, south of the Giant's Causeway.

Seeking an Armada wreck to salvage in the 1960s, the Belgian diver Robert Stenuit chose the *Girona*. Where exactly had she sunk? Stenuit spent many hours, 600 he says, examining ancient maps and documents. He also read old stories passed down from the vessel's nine survivors and the local people who had rescued them. The *Girona*, according to the stories, had sunk at midnight in a little cove near a bay significantly still named Port na Spaniagh.

Stenuit went to the area in 1967. He easily identified the bay and the other local landmarks such as Spanish Cave and Spanish Rock. His knowledge of winds and currents convinced him that the *Girona* had struck a submerged reef and plunged to her death on Lacada Point, scattering her treasure over a wide area.

He found the site of the wreck quickly. Swimming underwater he spotted cannon lying on the sea bed, half buried in sand. Following the vessel's likely track, he reached an underwater cave. It proved to be a treasure house. From it Stenuit and his friends brought out 1,161 gold and silver coins, eight gold

► At midnight on 26th October, 1588, the *Girona* struck a submerged reef off the coast of Northern Ireland. The vessel rolled over and was smashed into pieces on Lacada Point. The crew were tossed into the sea along with the coins, jewels and precious objects the ship was carrying. Four hundred years later, Robert Stenuit found the wreck.

Port na Spaniagh

IRELAND

▲ The *Girona* was wrecked near a place significantly called Port na Spaniagh. Robert Stenuit spent 600 hours researching the archives of five countries before he visited the site. He caught his first glimpse of the *Girona* treasure after only one hour's diving.

◄ One of Stenuit's divers finds a gold chain which had been hidden in the seaweed for nearly 400 years. Stenuit's team found eight gold chains. One was 2.5 metres long (8 ft) and weighed 1.8 kg (4 lbs). Other chains were found in pieces. The links were brought up to the surface and painstakingly joined together. The chains were originally worn for ornament but also served as a ready source of cash.

► Some of the treasure of the *Girona*. Amongst the gold objects were eleven lapis lazuli cameos set with pearls and a delicately engraved salamander set with rubies. In addition Stenuit found eight gold chains and twelve gold rings.

chains, gold and silver plate, silver forks and spoons, and golden ornaments. The treasure had no legal owner. Robert Stenuit arranged for it to be displayed at the Ulster Museum. It can be seen there together with the documents, maps and charts which Stenuit used in his search.

Proof that the wreck was the *Girona* came from the cannon balls that Stenuit salvaged. Their sizes exactly fitted the known calibres of the vessel's fifty cannon. More proof was supplied when some of the precious objects which had been salvaged were identified. Stenuit checked the Spanish records and identified the noblemen who could have been on board the *Girona* with their personal treasures.

A Malta Cross was found which bore part of the coat of arms of the *Girona*'s captain, Don Spinola. A gold ring engraved with the words 'Madame de Champagney 1524' was also found. This was traced to a young man who had drowned in the shipwreck. Madame de Champagney was his grandmother.

The golden galleons

From 1500, shortly after Columbus's discovery of the New World, until 1820 when the Spaniards were expelled from the Americas, the Spanish plate fleets sailed annually across the Atlantic. They carried a total of some £7,000,000,000 in gold, silver, minted coins and precious stones. This treasure was plundered from Mexico and Peru. About five per cent of this vast sum may have been lost by shipwreck and it is estimated that two per cent of this was never salvaged by the Spaniards. Many galleons were lost in hurricanes or by striking submerged reefs. Some were attacked by buccaneers or pirates.

Early losses forced the Spaniards to sail their ships in convoys. Each fleet, or *flota*, was accompanied by two powerful warships, a *capitana*, captained by the 'General', the commander of the fleet, and an *almiranta* in which sailed the admiral or navigator. Both vessels carried valuable cargo up to their laden capacity of 1,000 tonnes.

The general freighters, or urcas, sailed in the convoy carrying up to 800 tonnes of bullion according to their laden capacity. In addition to their official cargo, many captains carried unregistered freight as private trade. To stamp out this practice, which overloaded the ships, the royal officials in America forwarded to Spain an extra copy of each ship's cargo manifest, or inventory, on another ship.

Hundreds of thousands of such documents, including ships' logs and salvage records, were filed in the Archives of the Indies at Seville. The Archives provide an invaluable record of the *flotas* because they contain the cargo manifests not only of the vessels which reached Spain, but also of those that were wrecked on the way on the reef-strewn coasts of America and the Caribbean.

Owing to the prevailing easterly winds, the *flotas* were forced to adopt certain routes to reach the Atlantic from the Caribbean. Early on they sailed through the Old Bahamas Passage, skirting the northern coasts of what are now Haiti and Puerto Rico. Many vessels were wrecked on the submerged reefs which fringe the long stretch of the Bahamas.

In desperation the Spaniards adopted the equally dangerous New Bahamas Passage, between the Bahamas and the coast of Florida. From there the *flotas* sailed northwards to the Bermudas, where many were wrecked, before turning eastwards to Spain.

Only then could their captains breathe a sigh of relief, for the galleons and urcas were towering, unwieldy vessels, prey to the wind and waves. The galleon was a fast sailing ship designed to carry large cargoes. It had three or four masts which were fitted with large, square sails and lateen, or triangular, sails. There were usually two or three decks which carried heavy guns. The sides were straight, and the galleon stood high in the water. Its design caused it to be top-heavy despite the fact that ballast and stores were carried at the bottom of the hull. When it carried too much cargo, or too many men, the galleon became very unwieldy and was difficult to handle in storms.

Occasionally the *flotas* failed to sail and the accumulated riches piled up for shipment in the following year. This happened in 1715 and 1733 when the fleets suffered their worst disasters.

Several plate fleet wrecks have been located and their treasure, or part of it, recovered. There are many difficulties and hazards involved in the recovery of sunken treasure. The wreck may have become encased in coral or submerged by layers of mud and sand, so that its shape is difficult to recognize. Records of its location may have been lost.

Many wrecks are found by chance. Storms sweep away the sand, revealing tell-tale clues such as anchors, cannon and cannon balls. Many of these wrecks are identified by researching the Spanish archives or by following up local legends about the disasters.

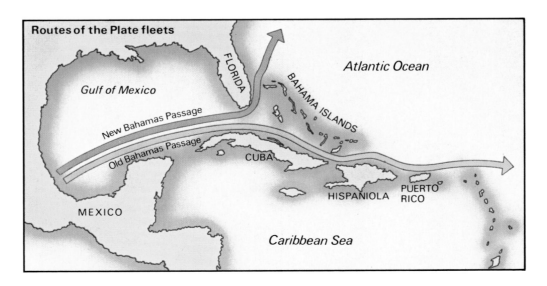

◄ The early Spanish treasure ships sailed for Spain through the Old Bahamas Passage which skirted the north of Cuba and Puerto Rico. This route contained dangerous submerged reefs and many vessels were wrecked. The later plate fleets followed the New Bahamas Passage which turned out to be equally dangerous. In addition to the reefs and shoals, this part of the American coast is plagued by violent storms and hurricanes. The Spaniards used skilled navigators, but the galleons were large and unwieldy, and difficult to control in stormy seas.

▲ The first treasure ships to sail for Spain often travelled alone. As trade developed between Spain and its colonies, pirates and foreign powers began to prey on the lone Spanish vessels. From the 1530s onwards, the Spaniards sailed their ships in convoy, protected by heavily-armed escorts. In addition to their valuable cargo, many of the ships carried the personal wealth of the officers and passengers. This included jewellery, and gold and silver plate.

◄ An early engraving of the Potosi silver mine in Bolivia. The mine lay in a high conical mountain in the Andes. It was discovered by an Indian slave in 1545. His Spanish master registered a claim with the authorities and work began on the mine. In 1572 Potosi acquired its own mint. Merchants flocked to the city to exploit the great wealth produced from the mine. Potosi was the biggest producer of silver in the Spanish colonies.

The salvage of the Concepcion

Stricken by a hurricane to the north of Cuba, the 1641 Plate Fleet was scattered. Ten ships were wrecked on the reefs of the Grand Bahama Bank. The *capitana* managed to survive and reached Spain with her huge cargo intact, but not so the *almiranta*.

Her admiral, the veteran navigator Juan de Villa-vincencio, aimed to get his battered vessel, the *Nuestra Senora de la Concepcion*, to Puerto Rico for repairs. Under Spanish regulations, his pilots could over-rule his decision on the route to take. In this case they did so and plunged the *Concepcion* amongst the dreaded Abrojos reefs. She struck and sank.

The two hundred survivors piled some gold and silver ingots on the reef (known since as the Silver Shoal) beside a pillar of coral. Over a million pounds worth of treasure remained within the wreck.

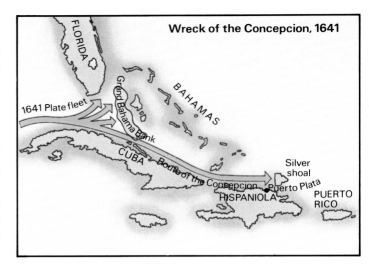

Wreck of the Concepcion, 1641

A Spanish treasure galleon

The Mediterranean galley propelled by oars, was replaced by the galleon for trans-Atlantic trade. Galleons were fast, strong sailing ships capable of carrying large cargoes. They were heavily protected against pirates and foreign vessels and carried cannon mounted between decks for stability. Galleons stood high in the water, with towering fo'c's'les and poops which helped to prevent boarding of the vessels by enemies. The fo'c's'les and poops were richly decorated with carvings. Stability was increased by keeping ballast stones, cargo and ship's stores at the bottom of the hull. But the weight of the masts and armament, and the height of the decks, made the galleons top-heavy and unwieldy. They were unseaworthy in the storms and hurricanes which often hit the Caribbean. Galleons had three or four masts. The foremast and mainmast carried square sails. The mizzen mast and bonaventure mizzen carried lateen, or triangular sails. The bonaventure mizzen was later left off, and the mizzen mast was made larger and given a square sail as well as a lateen sail.

1 Rudder
2 Treasure store
3 Poop
4 Bonaventure mizzen
5 Mizzen mast
6 Main mast
7 Fore mast
8 Bowsprit
9 Fo'c's'le
10 Ship's stores, cargo and ballast stones

▼ Most of the treasure carried by the plate fleets was kept in the hold. Divers without modern equipment could salvage treasure which had spilled out of a wreck but it was difficult to get into the hold.

▲ The 1641 Plate Fleet was struck by a hurricane at the beginning of its long voyage to Spain. One of the surviving vessels, the *Concepcion*, headed for Puerto Rico for repairs, but was wrecked on the Silver Shoal reef.

► William Phips was one of
the first professional
treasure hunters. He was an
enterprising ship's
carpenter from
Massachusetts. On a visit
to the Bahamas in 1683
Phips heard about the loss
of the *Concepcion* forty
years before, and the
attempts by others to find
her wreck. He decided to
join the hunt and sailed to
England to enlist the
support of King Charles II.

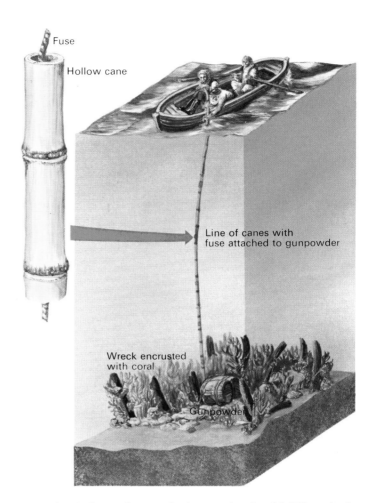

Fuse

Hollow cane

Line of canes with
fuse attached to gunpowder

Wreck encrusted
with coral

Gunpowder

◄ King Charles II, the
impecunious King of England,
had also heard the story of
the *Concepcion*. When Phips
arrived in England, he
gained an audience with the
King and easily persuaded
him to finance his
expedition to search for the
wreck, in return for a fourth
share of the treasure.

► Phips tried to blow open
the coral-encrusted hold of
the wreck. A fuse, encased
in waterproof canes, was
sent down to a barrel of
gunpowder. Each time the
fuse was lit it burned
through the canes and the
water extinguished the
spark.

One of the survivors met William Phips, a ship's
carpenter, in 1683 and told him the story. Phips took
himself to England where he succeeded in persuading
King Charles II to loan him a ship to recover the
treasure. He told the King that he alone knew the
location of the wreck.

By this audacious lie, Phips bluffed his way to
command the *Rose* in return for which the King was to
have a fourth of the treasure. Phips sailed to the Silver
Shoal. The ingots had been picked up by passing ships,
and Phips failed to find the pillar of coral, the old
sailor's guide to the wreck. He returned to England
and borrowed two larger ships from the King.

This time, Phips stayed at Puerto Plata on the north
coast of Hispaniola while the second vessel searched
for the wreck. While exploring the reefs, one of the
crew spotted a marine plant of extraordinary beauty
and dived into the sea to get it. He reappeared with the
exciting news that the plant lay surrounded by great
guns, sure sign of a wreck. In three days the crew
recovered 3,000 silver coins and many more ingots.

The captain marked the wreck with buoys and
returned to tell Phips of his news. They began 'fishing'
the wreck. Their divers brought up 37,538 pounds of
silver coins, 27,556 pounds of silver bullion, 347

pounds of silver plate and 26 pounds of gold. The whole
treasure amounted to £200,999 worth, perhaps worth
a million pounds today. Phips took £12,000 as his share
and was knighted.

But he was not satisfied. He believed that the bulk
of the treasure still lay within the vessel's hull, sealed
by layers of coral growth. But how was he to blast the
hull apart? Phips tried an ingenious experiment. His
divers lashed a barrel of gunpowder onto the wreck's
exposed deck. He hoped that the spark to explode it
could be carried down through the sea by a fuse
contained in a succession of hollow canes joined
together. But each time the fuse was lit it burned
through the cane tube and was extinguished by the
seawater.

Many modern treasure hunters believe that the bulk
of the treasure still lies within the *Concepcion*. Her hull
will have disintegrated by now and the treasure may be
found within the coral envelope which has encrusted
the wreck. Alexander Korganoff, a French Naval
diver, and Ed Link, the most famous of all underwater
archaeologists, have both visited the Silver Shoal.
Korganoff believes he has now located the wreck of the
Concepcion. But as far as we know, William Phips is
the only person to have raised treasure from the wreck.

The 1715 Plate Fleet

Some people believe that galleons three hundred years old can be found lying intact on the sea bed. In truth their wooden hulls would have rotted long ago. All that may remain are some anchors, cannon, cannon balls and ballast stones, and possibly treasure which became scattered when the vessels burst apart on contact with reefs. Even these clues may have become encrusted with coral or overlaid with sand. These inconvenient facts partly explain why it took so long to locate the wrecks of the 1715 Plate Fleet.

This fleet carried the amassed treasure of two years, valued in today's currency at thirty million pounds, and a collection of jewels intended by the Spanish king as a wedding gift for his queen.

A summer hurricane struck the heavily laden fleet of two warships and twelve freighters as it struggled up the New Bahamas Passage. The ships were cast on to the coast of Florida.

News of the disaster, the worst in the long history of the plate fleets, was brought by survivors to Havana in Cuba, from where the Spaniards despatched a salvage expedition. They recruited 280 Indian divers and during three years of work recovered over three million pounds worth of treasure. One hundred divers were drowned or eaten by sharks. Despite building a fort for protection, the Spaniards lost half a million pounds worth of treasure to the English pirate Henry Jennings.

The story of the disaster did not become forgotten, but its location did. That was the position in 1950 when Kip Wagner came to live at Wabasso on the Sebastian River. He heard stories that the fleet had been wrecked either 150 miles to the south or 60 miles to the north. But walking on the beach one day, he picked up a cluster of corroded silver coins. Cleaning disclosed

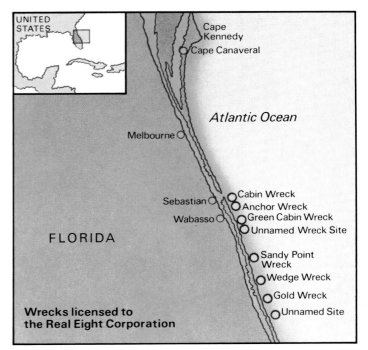

Wrecks licensed to the Real Eight Corporation

Map labels: UNITED STATES, Cape Kennedy, Cape Canaveral, Atlantic Ocean, Melbourne, Sebastian, Wabasso, FLORIDA, Cabin Wreck, Anchor Wreck, Green Cabin Wreck, Unnamed Wreck Site, Sandy Point Wreck, Wedge Wreck, Gold Wreck, Unnamed Site

▲ Kip Wagner and his colleagues located eight of the 1715 Plate Fleet wrecks. Before they began work they obtained an exclusive lease for each wreck site from the state of Florida.

▶ Indian divers salvaging the wrecks in the eighteenth century. The divers took down inverted buckets. When they ran out of breath they ducked under the buckets for more air.

their date as 1714. It set him wondering where exactly the Plate Fleet of 1715 had foundered.

Wagner discussed the problem with his friend, Dr Kip Kelso. As a result, Kelso visited the Library of Congress in Washington where he asked for the earliest history of Florida. In the rare books section he was shown a book published in 1775 written by the mapmaker Bernard Romans. It contained a map of the coast. Opposite the Sebastian River was the remark 'Here perished the Admiral commanding the Plate Fleet of 1715'.

Thus the fleet had perished on the shore close to Wagner's house. He and Kelso were not yet satisfied. They sent for three thousand microfilmed documents, including each ship's cargo manifest and the results of the salvage expedition, from the Archives of the Indies housed at Seville in Spain.

Wagner later paddled out from the beach and spotted clusters of cannon on the sea bed. They had been exposed by a storm which had washed away the sand. Wagner and Kelso recruited a team of skindivers and formed the Real Eight Syndicate. Between 1958 and 1964 the Syndicate raised treasure from the wrecks worth more than one million dollars. Salvage work will continue until the last wreck has been examined.

◀ A painting of a Spanish plate fleet. The towering unwieldy galleons were prey to hurricanes and storms.

Salvage of the 1715 Plate Fleet
in the eighteenth century

► The treasure was hauled
up to the surface in vessels
attached to a line.

◄ The Indian divers carried
a heavy stone to enable them
to sink quickly down to the
wreck. They would release
the stone at the bottom and
search for treasure until
their breath gave out after
3 or 4 minutes.

▲ Some divers were taught
to use an upturned cask or
bucket as a diving bell.

The Vigo Bay galleons

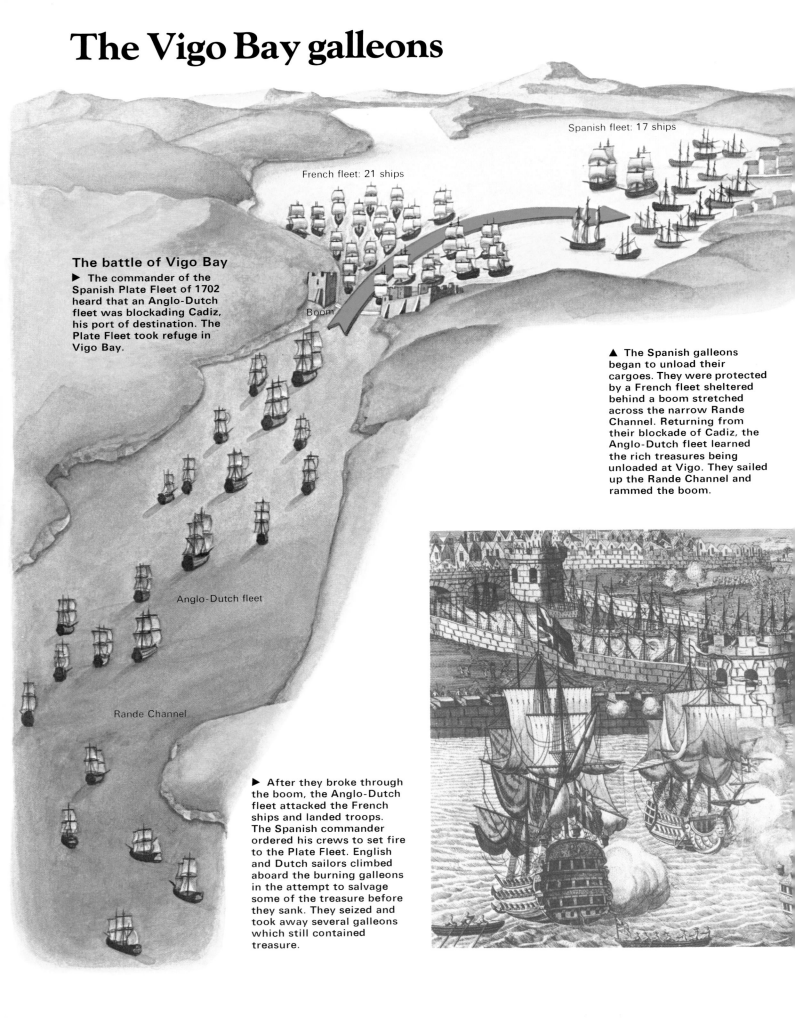

Spanish fleet: 17 ships

French fleet: 21 ships

The battle of Vigo Bay

▶ The commander of the Spanish Plate Fleet of 1702 heard that an Anglo-Dutch fleet was blockading Cadiz, his port of destination. The Plate Fleet took refuge in Vigo Bay.

Boom

▲ The Spanish galleons began to unload their cargoes. They were protected by a French fleet sheltered behind a boom stretched across the narrow Rande Channel. Returning from their blockade of Cadiz, the Anglo-Dutch fleet learned the rich treasures being unloaded at Vigo. They sailed up the Rande Channel and rammed the boom.

Anglo-Dutch fleet

Rande Channel

▶ After they broke through the boom, the Anglo-Dutch fleet attacked the French ships and landed troops. The Spanish commander ordered his crews to set fire to the Plate Fleet. English and Dutch sailors climbed aboard the burning galleons in the attempt to salvage some of the treasure before they sank. They seized and took away several galleons which still contained treasure.

Following a three year gap in sailing, the Spaniards shipped large quantities of treasure from Mexico and Peru in the Plate Fleet of 1702. During the voyage the fleet's commander learned that the port of destination, Cadiz, was being blockaded by an Anglo-Dutch fleet. The commander took his ships to northern Spain to avoid the blockade and entered Vigo Bay in safety. The Spanish galleons rode at anchor while unloading part of their cargo.

In the meantime the Anglo-Dutch fleet abandoned its blockade of Cadiz and began sailing home. On the way, one of the English ships called into the port of

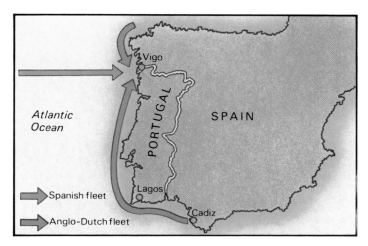

Lagos, in Portugal. The ship's chaplain went ashore and visited a bar. There he overheard the word 'galleons' and listened intently. He learnt that the plate fleet had escaped into Vigo Bay.

When he returned with the news, the Anglo-Dutch fleet joined the squadrons commanded by Admiral Sir Cloudesley Shovell, which had been patrolling the north-western corner of Spain. Together they sailed into Vigo Bay and rammed the boom erected by the Spaniards. They sank eleven galleons, some of which had been set on fire by their crews. The English and Dutch collected 2,596 kilos (5,720 pounds) of silver and 3,500 silver coins.

One Spanish galleon was captured intact and escorted out of the harbour by the *Monmouth*. But at the mouth of the harbour, the galleon struck a submerged reef and sank. It is thought that she was carrying a large proportion of the plate fleet's treasure.

The sinking of the plate fleet launched the greatest treasure hunt ever to take place in Europe. But how many of the sunken galleons had landed their cargoes before the Anglo-Dutch fleet swept in? That question has been argued for 250 years. Documents are cited to prove that the galleons carried twenty million pounds worth of treasure. At least a third of that is thought to have been unloaded. Does the rest of the treasure lie at the bottom of Vigo Bay?

Attempts to salvage the treasure began in 1740. In 1825 a Scotsman, Isaac Dickson, anchored his sloop in the bay. He made several dives and then vanished with a reported fortune. In the nineteenth century, Jules Verne wrote a fictional account of treasure salvage in his book *Twenty Thousand Leagues Under the Sea*. He based his story on the search for the Vigo Bay galleons.

The American engineer, John S. Potter, Jr., went to the bay in 1955 attracted by the reports of vast treasures to be salvaged there, but found that the galleons lay under deep mud. He decided to concentrate his efforts on the *Monmouth's* prize, the galleon which had sunk at the mouth of the bay. He ruled out the traditional site of her loss first of all. Research at the Public Record Office in London disclosed that her draught had been 6 metres (21 feet). This eliminated the submerged reef 7 metres (24 feet) below the surface on which, according to tradition, she had perished.

By further research, Potter concluded that the galleon had foundered on another reef, which had been incorrectly charted in 1702. After the impact, the ship would have heeled over into deep water. At this point the sea was 91 metres (300 feet) deep, beyond the range of skindivers lacking special gear. Potter abandoned his search in 1958 but he hopes to return to salvage the wreck. The rich galleon lies, he believes, under tons of sand and rubble. To recover her treasure would be a costly undertaking.

The Association: a naval blunder

Following the battle at Vigo Bay, Sir Cloudesley Shovell led his fleet home to England in September 1717. He sailed in the *Association*, a three-decker of 1,459 tonnes. The ships reached the entrance to the English Channel on 22nd October. Because of the murky weather, the vessels were navigating 'blind' without the aid of the stars.

The captains of the twenty-one vessels were called to the Admiral's ship. There they admitted that they did not know the position of the fleet. Some thought they were off the French coast. One declared they were approaching the Scilly Isles at England's south-western extremity. He alone was right. The four leading ships, led by the *Association*, plunged ahead in the rising storm and gathering darkness. Suddenly they struck the Gilstone Reef, the sea-washed rocks to the south-east of the island of St. Mary's. Shovell, his four captains and two thousand seamen were drowned. According to a Cornish legend, Shovell survived the shipwreck but was murdered by a local woman who found him on the beach and stole his rings.

No attempt was made to salvage the wrecks at the time, but in 1749 a meticulously drawn chart of the reefs was made by an Admiralty hydrographer. A particular reef had been locally named 'the Shovell', possibly a guide to the wreck.

A team from the Royal Naval Air Service Sub-Aqua Club attempted salvage operations in 1964. They dived in rough seas and strong currents and brought up a cannon which matched cannon of the period. Twenty more cannon and an anchor bar were hoisted up later. Although the salvage of these cannon appeared to indicate the position of the *Association*, nothing more was found except a few coins. Their discovery led to exaggerated tales of vast treasure trove lying on the sea bed. The *Association*, it was glibly stated, carried Shovell's gold plate and the trading profits of British merchants in Portugal.

Roland Morris, a Penzance restaurant owner and keen diver, also took up the challenge. One of the members of his syndicate, John Lipton, related how he first spotted treasure. After shinning down a narrow underwater rock chimney, Lipton stumbled on to 'a carpet of silver and gold – thousands and thousands of coins, guineas, crowns and pieces of eight'. Morris and his friends brought up 1,500 of these valuable coins. The treasure is the property of the Crown which rewards finders with a statutory half share of the proceeds.

Another discovery, a silver plate bearing Admiral Shovell's family crest, has created a legal issue. A woman who traces her descent from the Admiral claims that the treasure is hers by right. The Admiral's gold plate, if it is recovered, would be worth a million pounds today.

▲ Some of the bronze cannon raised from the wreck being cleaned on the quayside at St Mary's.

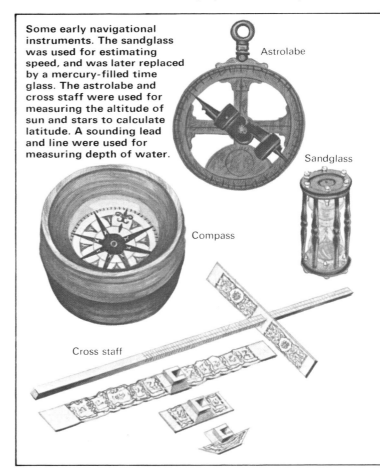

Some early navigational instruments. The sandglass was used for estimating speed, and was later replaced by a mercury-filled time glass. The astrolabe and cross staff were used for measuring the altitude of sun and stars to calculate latitude. A sounding lead and line were used for measuring depth of water.

Astrolabe

Sandglass

Compass

Cross staff

Until the invention of the ship's chronometer in 1735 by John Harrison, sailors could only estimate longitude by dead reckoning, checked by astronomical observation. A log attached to a knotted line was dropped from the stern of the ship. The number of knots which passed overboard in 28 seconds gave the speed of the ship. Currents and tides could make this measurement very inaccurate.

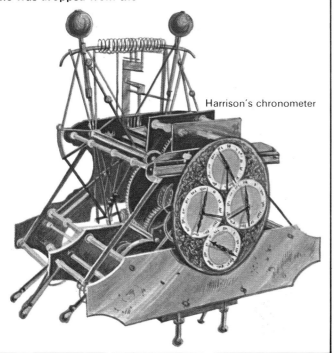

Harrison's chronometer

▲ A diver investigating the wreck of the *Association*. The rocks and dangerous currents of the Gilstone Reef make diving particularly hazardous.

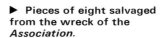

▶ Pieces of eight salvaged from the wreck of the *Association*.

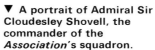

▼ A portrait of Admiral Sir Cloudesley Shovell, the commander of the *Association*'s squadron.

A triumph of analysis: *Le Chameau*

On the night of 26th August, 1725, the French pay-ship *Le Chameau* was approaching the harbour of Louisburg, the fortress guarding the seaway to Quebec. At the height of a raging storm, the ship struck a submerged reef. Within a few minutes all the 316 people on board were dead, and her cargo of 300,000 silver and gold coins had been scattered on the sea bed. The local fishermen were awakened by the rending crash, but could do nothing until dawn broke. The dangerous reef on which *Le Chameau* perished has been known ever since as Chameau Rock.

Alex Storm and his partners, Dave MacEachern and Harvey MacLeod, decided to search for the wreck of *Le Chameau* in 1965. The only clue to its where-abouts was Chameau Rock. Storm researched the French archives. He found a detailed inventory of the coins shipped, as well as the vessel's plan and dimensions, in the Naval Museum in Paris. He noted that she had carried fifty cannon of various calibres. The discovery of these cannon would provide strong clues to the wreck's course after striking the reef.

Before beginning their search, the partners acquired a licence from the Canadian government. This gave them exclusive rights for three years in return for ten per cent of any treasure they might find.

Between them they bought an old fishing boat and sailed to their starting point, Chameau Rock. Skin-diving in that area was particularly hazardous owing to the presence in summer of giant basking sharks. These sharks are not known to be man-eaters, but the divers didn't want to take any chances.

Alex Storm's knowledge of tides and currents helped him to estimate the course taken by *Le Chameau* after striking the reef. The ship had split into several sections, depositing cannon and anchors as each part careered shorewards. The vessel had then struck another reef where the remnants of the hull were torn off. The cannon and anchors marked the trail to be followed.

To ensure that no part of the sea bed would be overlooked, the partners constructed a grid of buoys anchored to bottles filled with cement. They found the

How *Le Chameau* sank

1. *Le Chameau* hit a partly submerged reef which ripped open the wooden hull.

2. The vessel keeled over and capsized in the raging waters. No one on the ship survived.

3. Anchors and cannon and ballast fell into the sea and the vessel righted itself.

◄ Alex Storm with his partners, Dave MacEachern and Harvey Macleod. Storm was an experienced diver working for a salvage company in Canada when he first heard the story of *Le Chameau* in 1961. In 1965 he decided to hunt for the wreck and recruited MacEachern, an amateur diver, and Macleod, a sailor.

► Despite his careful research, Storm was lucky to find the treasure. Usually an ancient wreck is traced by mounds of ballast stones, cannon and timber on the sea bed. But *Le Chameau* timbers had disintegrated and the lead shot she carried as ballast lay hidden beneath the sand.

first anchor 213 metres (700 ft) from the reef. Further on they salvaged 44 cannon, and then another. The last cannon was wedged between rocks.

From a crevice, Alex Storm's eye caught the gleam of gold. Below him, spread out on the rocky sea bed, was the treasure of *Le Chameau*. Months of patient research and diving in icy waters had brought their reward. Storm picked up a gold coin and looked at it closely. It bore the profile of King Louis XV and the date 1725. He looked up and saw that Dave Mac-Eachern had found another batch of coins nearby.

Altogether the partners raised 11,000 pieces of silver, 2,000 Louis d'Or coins, silver candlesticks, spoons, forks, knives, swords, pewter dishes, pottery and glassware. So far they had kept their discoveries secret, but now they had recovered most of the treasure they took it to a numismatist who valued it at $700,000 (about £400,000).

Commenting on his discovery, Alex Storm said that he and his partners were very lucky to have found the wreck. That may be, but they went about it the right way – thinking first and diving later.

4. The vessel was tossed on to another submerged reef. The upper deck and the sides of the vessel were ripped away.

5. The remains of *Le Chameau* drifted through the foaming waves.

6. Finally the bottom of the hull fell away and the treasure sank on to the sea bed.

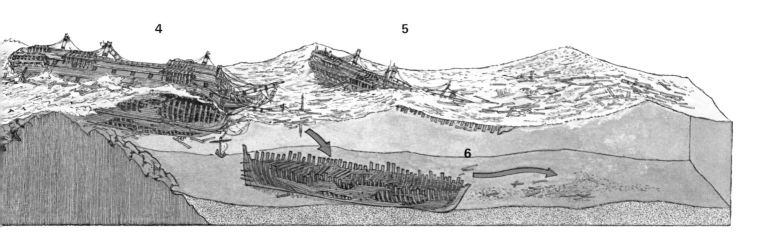

A technological feat: the *Egypt*

The English liner *Egypt* was holed in a collision with the French steamer *Seine* and sank in the Bay of Biscay on 20th May, 1927. She carried a cargo of gold bars destined for India, valued at over a million pounds. Could this great treasure be salvaged? That seemed improbable for the vessel lay at a depth of 122 metres (400 ft), far below the limits of steel-helmeted and rubber-suited divers. They would be crushed to death by the water pressure long before they reached that depth.

The Italian salvage firm Sorima thought the *Egypt* was worth a try. They made a contract with the ship's insurers under which they would keep forty per cent of what they salvaged. But first they needed to locate the wreck. This in itself was a fearful task. The *Egypt* had sunk in open sea out of sight of land and thus no navigational 'fixes' could be made from the coast. Owing to fog, the ship's course had not been accurately charted and the four miles an hour current could have increased the error. The survivors were able only to indicate an area covering twenty square miles.

The crews of Sorima's salvage vessels, the *Artiglio* and the *Rostro*, were forced to adopt the time-consuming exercise of sweeping the sea bed with a long cable weighed down with lead. As the area was a veritable graveyard of wrecks, the cable was certain to locate several. The problem was to identify the *Egypt* from amongst them.

The *Artiglio* drew a blank in the north-western corner of the area. The sweep was transferred to the south-eastern corner where several wrecks were located. When the cable caught on the wreck of the *Egypt*, the *Artiglio* was nearly dragged under. The crew lowered a grab to the wreck. It brought up a curved shaft of rusty steel. The shaft looked like part of a davit used for lowering a boat. The team of divers

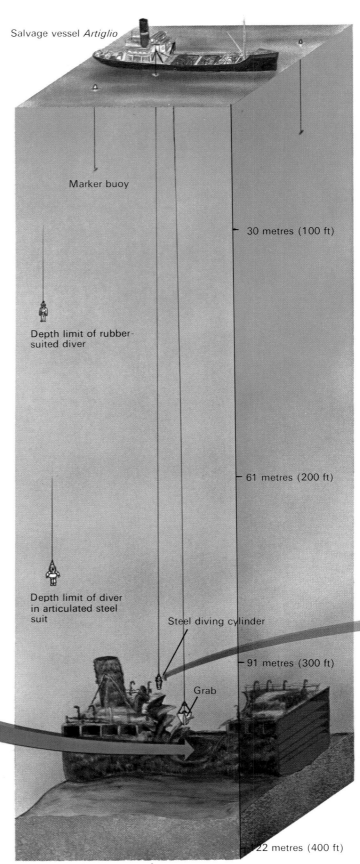

Salvage vessel *Artiglio*

Marker buoy

30 metres (100 ft)

Depth limit of rubber-suited diver

61 metres (200 ft)

Depth limit of diver in articulated steel suit

Steel diving cylinder

91 metres (300 ft)

Grab

122 metres (400 ft)

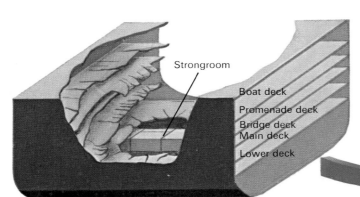

Strongroom

Boat deck
Promenade deck
Bridge deck
Main deck
Lower deck

Cross-section of the *Egypt*'s hull showing extent of demolition needed

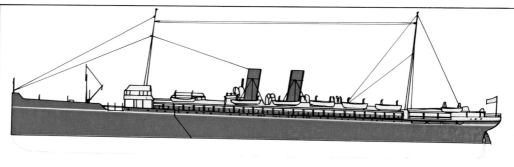

▶ The *Egypt* was a P & O liner built in 1897. She was 152 metres (500 ft) long. When the wreck was found the decks and rigging had disintegrated and the whole ship was covered in a growth of brown weed.

Steel diving cylinder

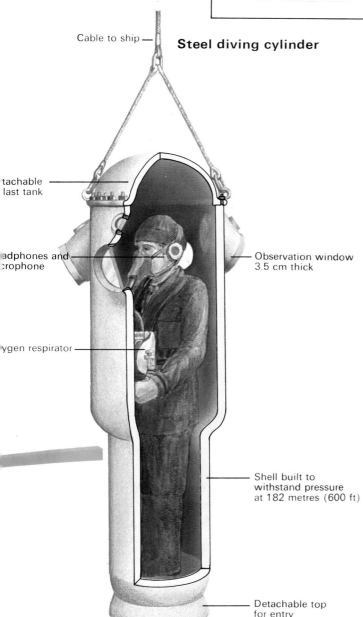

Cable to ship —

tachable last tank

adphones and crophone

ygen respirator

— Observation window 3.5 cm thick

— Shell built to withstand pressure at 182 metres (600 ft)

— Detachable top for entry

▲ A diver inside the steel diving cylinder which was lowered from the salvage vessel by cable. The diver was equipped with a telephone headpiece and breathing mask.

▶ Gold bars from the *Egypt* on the deck of the *Artiglio*. They were brought up by grabs lowered by the salvage vessel. The diver in the steel cylinder directed operations by telephone.

examined the *Egypt*'s plan which they had obtained from its owners. The height of the davit exactly fitted the steel shaft. The *Egypt* had been found.

To prepare for this hoped-for result, the Sorima company had built a steel diving cylinder, with windows and searchlights, capable of descending to a depth of 183 metres (600 ft). Sealed within it an observer, linked to the *Artiglio* by telephone, could direct the lowering of grabs from a derrick on the vessel's deck.

The *Egypt*'s plan showed that the gold bars had been stored in a narrow hold three decks down. These decks would have to be demolished before the grab could reach the gold bars. It took thirty working days, spread over four months, to tear away the decks by demolition charges.

The grab plunged into the wreck's treasure vault on 22nd June, 1931. It brought up seventeen gold bars. The next scoop brought up eleven gold bars and seventeen gold sovereigns. When salvage operations finished, ninety-nine per cent of the *Egypt*'s treasure had been brought to the surface. The Sorima Company gained nearly £600,000. Seven gold bars and about ten thousand gold sovereigns remain within the wreck. They lie buried under a welter of iron rust, too unprofitable to salvage.

Legendary Treasures

Pirates' gold

During the seventeenth and eighteenth centuries many pirates lurked in the Caribbean, attracted by the wealth of the Spaniards.

In 1658, England seized the island of Jamaica. The new governors of the island adopted a group of pirates known as the buccaneers for their 'navy'. With their admiral, Henry Morgan, the buccaneers set up their headquarters at Port Royal. They sailed in fleets through the Caribbean and the Spanish Main, sacking towns and cities. When England and Spain made a treaty in 1670, the buccaneers were expelled. They became lone pirates, sailing the seven seas and preying upon the ships of all nations.

Men such as William Kidd and Blackbeard Teach were true pirates, men who needed to conceal their plunder. Some buried their treasure and a few drew charts or left clues to the places of concealment. But did they return to lift their caches?

Blackbeard Teach was a true story-book pirate. He came from Bristol in England, and turned pirate in 1710. His vessel, the *Queen Anne's Revenge*, was armed with forty guns. Teach quickly gained a reputation for brutality. He would sometimes maroon his victims on desolate coral cays, or force them to 'walk the plank'.

Teach's victims appealed to the Governor of Virginia who sent the Royal Naval Lieutenant Maynard to capture him. Maynard caught up with the *Revenge* in an inlet and fought Teach to the finish. He sailed back to Virginia with Blackbeard's head swinging from the bowsprit.

In 1717, some time before his death, Teach landed a heavy iron-bound chest on Plum Island. Six men buried it in a deep hole on the beach and then Teach shot each man, so leaving no eyewitness to disclose his hiding place.

On Christmas Day, 1928, two fishermen were crossing the same beach. They came across a freshly dug hole. Its sandy floor bore the imprint of an iron-bound chest and from the hole ran a trail to the nearby inlet. Someone had discovered the secret of the hiding place and dug up Blackbeard's treasure.

Did Captain William Kidd leave a great treasure? This is believed by many treasure hunters who have sought it all over the world. Innumerable treasure sites are attributed to him.

In 1691 Kidd was a rich merchant who owned his own vessel. At the age of fifty-four he craved adventure. His chance came when he was persuaded by influential backers to accept the command of the *Adventure Galley*. The ship was to be used for hunting out the pirates who infested the Indian Ocean. When recruiting his crew, Kidd was forced to take on rogues and deserters, many of whom were the very pirates he had been ordered to capture. They were recruited on the "no prey, no pay" principle, whereby they only earned money if they took prizes.

Inevitably his men forced Kidd to turn pirate. In the Indian Ocean he captured the *Quedah Merchant*, an Armenian vessel, and seized her cargo. Technically the ship was a 'fair prize' because she sailed under the protection of the French flag while England and France were at war.

Kidd sailed the *Quedah Merchant* to the West Indies where he learnt that he had been accused of piracy. Before his arrest he secretly buried £14,000 in gold bars and coins on Gardiner's Island, New York. He disclosed his hiding place before his execution for piracy, and the treasure was dug up by the government. Kidd's remaining wealth, £6,000, was seized by the Crown and used to build the Greenwich Hospital for Seamen.

The day before his execution at Wapping in 1701, Kidd sought a last minute reprieve by offering to lead an expedition to recover the *Quedah Merchant*'s valuable cargo. But the government refused his offer. They knew that the *Quedah Merchant* had been looted and burned by other pirates during the time Kidd was in prison.

◀ A pirate being hanged at Wapping. The rewards of piracy could be great, but punishment was severe.

◀ Henry Morgan became one of the leaders of the buccaneers. He was knighted by Charles II and made governor of Jamaica.

▲ In 1671 the buccaneers raided the Spanish city of Panama and carried away the great wealth of its inhabitants.

▲ An engraving of Captain Kidd with his men. According to popular myth, Kidd's treasure is still waiting to be found, but in fact it was all recovered before his death.

◀ Blackbeard Teach treated his victims with great cruelty. He amassed a vast amount of treasure and buried it on Plum Island before he died.

▶ The trial of William Kidd for piracy and murder, in 1701. His influential backers deserted him. He was found guilty and hanged.

The legend of Cocos Island

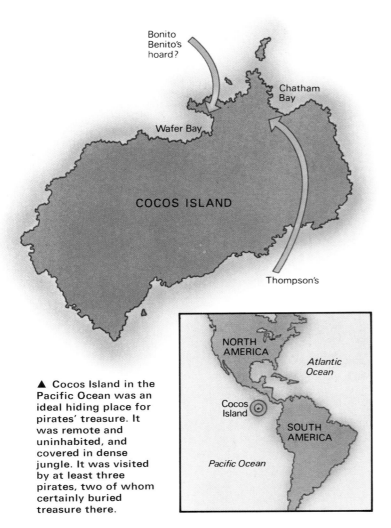

▲ Cocos Island in the Pacific Ocean was an ideal hiding place for pirates' treasure. It was remote and uninhabited, and covered in dense jungle. It was visited by at least three pirates, two of whom certainly buried treasure there.

Three pirates are reputed to have concealed vast treasures on Cocos Island which lies in the Pacific, 350 miles from the coast of Costa Rica. One man, John Keating, is believed to have taken great wealth from the island. Inspired by his legendary success, countless treasure hunters have visited the island but they have come away empty-handed.

This may be due to several reasons. Landslides on the island have obliterated landmarks, clues have become confused, and information relating to three separate treasures appears to have merged into one story.

The Cocos story is typical of treasure concealments. Truth becomes distorted by hearsay. Stories become more inaccurate at each telling. There are often no documents to check them by. As a result the Cocos treasures will probably stay concealed for ever unless they are found by accident. That is unlikely because the island is remote and uninhabited. It is said that only suckers search for treasure on Cocos Island.

The earliest cache on Cocos is supposed to have been made by the English pirate Edward Davis in the seventeenth century. He is said to have landed seven boatloads of booty.

Some years later another pirate, called Bonito Benito, is said to have brought eleven million dollars worth of plunder to the island and concealed his share in a cave. With him he had a man named Thompson.

In the same year, another man called Thompson is supposed to have hidden treasure on the island and this has led to much confusion. The second Thompson was captain of a ship called the *Mary Dear*. In 1821, Lima, the capital of Peru, was besieged by revolu-

▲ August Gissler first visited the island in 1889. He had been given clues to a treasure hoard by a seaman who claimed his grandfather had sailed with Benito Bonito. Gissler returned to the island in 1891 and stayed for seventeen years. He obtained a licence for exclusive rights to the treasure from the president of Costa Rica, but he found only thirty-three gold coins.

▲ In 1929, Captain Mangell, a French yachtsman, reached the island armed with a map which he had found in Australia. This was apparently one of the maps left by Keating when he died. He anchored his yacht offshore and went into the entrance of a cave which was free from water at low tide. Mangell began to dig in the floor of the cave, but the rising tide forced him to leave.

tionaries. The Spanish officials and priests loaded their vast treasure onto the *Mary Dear* for shipment to Spain. Once it was safely aboard, Thompson seized the treasure and set sail for Cocos Island, where he buried it.

Thompson and his mate, James Forbes, were later arrested and forced to return to Cocos to reveal their hiding place, but they escaped into the jungle.

Around 1844, a carpenter named John Keating met a seaman called Thompson who gave him a map of Cocos Island. Keating visited the island with a partner called Boag and eventually returned to the mainland loaded with gold. Boag had disappeared. Keating said he had found the treasure hidden in a cave and that Boag had drowned in a stream whilst trying to cross it loaded down with treasure.

▲ This aerial photograph of Cocos Island shows the dense forest which would soon cover up clues to any possible treasure site.

▲ Keating was the first person to search for treasure on Cocos Island. He came away with masses of gold but without his partner, who had mysteriously disappeared. Keating left copies of his map to three people when he died a few years later.

◄ The late Sir Malcolm Campbell, the racing motorist and world speed record holder, visited Cocos in 1926 to search for treasure. He stayed on the island for several days, but found nothing.

▲ A man called Peter Bergmans also visited Cocos in 1929. On his return, he claimed to have found Bonito's treasure cave. It contained gold, silver, church ornaments and large chests filled with jewels. He also found the skeleton of a man . perhaps that of Boag, Keating's partner, who had been left to die in the cave. But on his return to the island, Bergmans could not find the cave again.

▲ In 1939, James Forbes turned up on Cocos with his brother. He was the great-grandson of the mate of the *Mary Dear* who had hidden the Lima treasure on the island. They spent several weeks digging up the beach at a spot no-one had previously thought of as a possible hiding place for the Lima treasure. But the brothers left the island without finding anything.

The Seychelles mystery

'Find my treasure who can!' These were the last words of the French pirate Olivier le Vasseur before he was hanged in 1730. From his hand fluttered several pieces of paper. One of the spectators seized them. They included a cryptogram, a message in symbolic writing, which appeared to be a set of directions.

Little is known about le Vasseur, who was nick-named *La Buze* (The Buzzard). He gained some spectacular prizes including a Portuguese vessel and an Arab ship. Both vessels were rich in gold, silver and precious jewels. Their capture alerted the French authorities in the Indian Ocean and le Vasseur was captured and hanged for piracy.

According to one story, his papers were found by a French family named Savy who lived on the island of Mahé in the Seychelles. They thought the documents referred to Mahé and indicated a treasure concealment on the beach at Bel Ombre. But no-one could interpret the clues.

That was the situation in 1949 when Reginald Herbert Cruise-Wilkins visited the Seychelles on holiday. He went to Bel Ombre where he met Mrs Savy. She told him the story of the documents and showed him some rocks on which had been drawn several strange markings.

Cruise-Wilkins became convinced that the rock markings and the cryptogram were clues to le Vasseur's treasure. Together they formed a rough code, if it could be interpreted.

▲ Cruise-Wilkins on the beach at Bel Ombre. This man has spent over twenty years of his life searching the beach for the treasure buried by a French pirate.

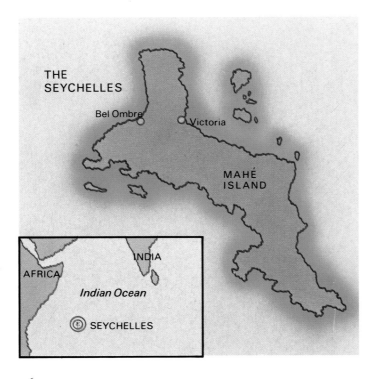

▲ After le Vasseur's death, it is thought that his documents were copied several times by eager treasure hunters who responded to his challenge.

Above is one version of his cryptogram. Cruise-Wilkins believes that le Vasseur based his clues on the Twelve Labours of Hercules, and the constellations.

Cruise-Wilkins began to decipher the cryptogram and came to the conclusion that it was based on stories from Greek mythology and some knowledge of astronomy. Following the directions of the cryptogram, he began to excavate on the beach at Bel Ombre. His first attempt revealed a statue of Andromeda buried in the sand. He dug at other sites, where buried objects and carvings corresponded to clues in the cryptogram. The buried objects included a horse's skeleton and cattle bones, and the carvings included the hoofprints of a stag or hind. These findings began to take on a pattern in Cruise-Wilkins's mind. They appeared to be symbols of the Twelve Labours of Hercules.

Further excavations led him finally to the site of the Twelfth Labour, symbolized on the beach by a rock carving of Cerberus, the dog who guarded the entrance to Hades. Here, Cruise-Wilkins believes, lies the site of le Vasseur's treasure. Whether his interpretations are correct is anyone's guess. They suggest that le Vasseur was a very well-educated pirate.

Cruise-Wilkins believes that the treasure lies in a cave hidden below the huge boulders on which Cerberus is carved. Although he is so near to the legendary treasure, Cruise-Wilkins cannot afford to excavate. He would need expensive equipment capable of removing tons of rocks to reach the cave.

▶ Cruise-Wilkins with one of the clues – a double stone symbolizing one of the labours of Hercules. Beside him is a rock with carvings giving another clue.

The Labours of Hercules

1 The Nemean lion. Hercules choked it to death and wore its pelt as armour and its head as a helmet.
2 Lernaean hydra. Hercules severed its immortal head and buried it under a rock.
3 Ceryneian hind. Hercules hunted it until he captured it alive.
4 Erymanthian boar. Hercules bound it with chains in order to capture it alive.
5 Stables Of Augeias. Hercules diverted two rivers to clean the stables.
6 Stymphalian birds. Hercules shook rattles to terrorize these man-eating birds. He then shot them down.
7 Cretan bull. Hercules struggled single-handed with this fire-breathing monster.
8 Mares of Diomedes. Hercules fed them with the flesh of their master to make them docile.
9 Hippolyte's girdle. Hercules killed the Queen of the Amazons and captured her golden girdle.
10 Cattle of Geryon. Hercules shot Geryon sideways with a single arrow through his three bodies and won his cattle.
11 Apples of the Hesperides. Hercules took the world on his shoulders while Atlas brought him the golden apples.
12 Cerberus. Hercules captured Cerberus while protected by his lion's pelt.

El Dorado

The legend of El Dorado, the gilded one, grew rapidly after the Spaniards reached South America around 1500. High amongst the peaks of the Andes, in what is now Colombia, lay a crater which contained Lake Quatavita. Near the lake lived a peaceful people known as the Chibcha. Each new chief of the Chibcha celebrated his accession to kingship with a ceremony on the lake. The chief's body was covered in resinous gum and then a layer of gold dust. He was carried on a raft to the centre of the lake where he plunged into the water. His subjects and priests cast gold and precious stones such as emeralds into the lake.

The story of El Dorado, the gilded one, reached the ears of the gold-hungry Spaniards, and became magnified in the telling. Gold was as common as dirt in the land of the golden one, they believed. The legend encouraged the Spanish conquistadors to make many expeditions into the interior of South America.

One of the first expeditions, led by Gonzalo Jimenez de Quesada, reached the lake in 1538. Quesada had collected a vast amount of gold and emeralds from the tribes he encountered on the way. He found more treasure on the shallow edge of Lake Quatavita and attempted to drain the lake, but was unsuccessful.

Forty years later another expedition attempted to drain the lake. Using a vast army of native indians, they cut a gap more than 30 metres (100 ft) long through the crater wall surrounding the lake. Water gushed out and reduced the lake's level by five metres (15 ft). This exposed numerous gold objects, which have been valued at over £100,000, and an emerald which was sold for over £45,000. A disastrous landslide ended the treasure hunt.

In the nineteenth century, Charles Cockrane, an English naval captain, became interested in the legend. He calculated that £120,000,000 worth of treasure still lay at the bottom of the lake. He based his improbable estimate on a story told by descendants of the Inca kings. According to the story 'as much gold as fifty men could carry' had been thrown into the lake at the time of the Spanish Conquest.

Cockrane's notes were discovered in 1903 by an English company which succeeded in partly draining Lake Quatavita by boring a tunnel through the crater wall. They extracted from the muddy depths golden snakes, bowls, a warrior's helmet and several emeralds. When the engineers returned to the lake the next day, they found that the heat of the sun had baked the mud as hard as concrete. While they were away trying to find drills, the lake filled up with water again.

Several modern treasure hunting syndicates have announced plans for draining the lake. One group sent down skindivers, but their work was hampered by low visibility and the great depth of the lake. The fabulous treasure still defies those who hope to recover it.

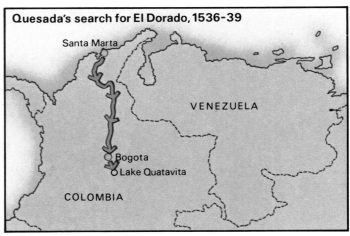

Quesada's search for El Dorado, 1536-39

Santa Marta

VENEZUELA

Bogota
Lake Quatavita

COLOMBIA

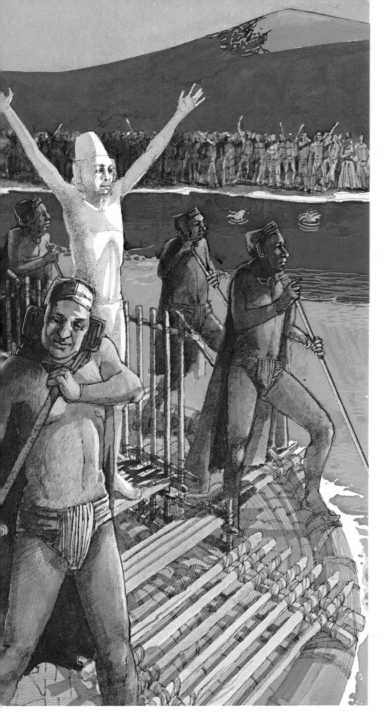

◄ As the sun rose above Lake Quatavita, a raft pushed off from the bank. On it stood El Dorado, the gilded one, with his arms stretched out towards the rising sun. His six oarsmen guided the raft to the dark waters at the centre of the lake. At the climax of the ceremony, El Dorado dived into the lake, offering the gold on his body to the gods. His subjects waiting on the banks threw their offerings of gold and precious jewels into the water.

Below left: a gold mask from Colombia, one of many precious objects found near Lake Quatavita.

▲ A gold mask made by the Chibcha. The Chibcha were a peaceful people with a well-organized system of agriculture. They were not as advanced as the Incas who lived to the south, and not much is known about them today.

▼ A human-like figure made of solid gold and gold wire by Chibcha craftsmen. The Chibcha, like many other Indians in South America, were conquered by the Spaniards. The Spaniards were impressed by the amount of gold, silver and precious stones possessed by the Indians. They seized the wealth of the Indians and made expeditions to search for more.

Lobengula's hidden hoard

▲ A Matabele warrior. The Matabele, or Ndebele, were related to the Zulus. Like the Zulus, the Matabele had a highly-trained army. The warriors fought with assegais (spears) and shields.

◄ Lobengula, chief of the Matabele, with some of his attendants. He was renowned as an able but despotic ruler. With the advance of British troops in 1892, Lobengula decided to hide his wealth. This consisted of raw gold, ivory, uncut diamonds and bags of sovereigns.

◄ A scene from the Matabele War of 1893. In the late nineteenth century European powers were competing with each other for control of Africa. In the face of Dutch, German and Portuguese expansion, the British annexed Matabeleland. It became part of Rhodesia, despite two rebellions by the Matabele.

▶ If Lobengula's hoard is ever found, it may become the centre of a legal wrangle. There has already been a dispute over the ownership of the treasure. Among the claimants could be the descendants of the Matabele, the De Beers Mining Company, and the government of Mozambique.

Lobengula was the Chief of the Matabele tribe in 1892 when the British invaded the land they later named Rhodesia. Foreseeing the inevitable subjection of his people and the end of his rule, Lobengula gathered his riches together. His wealth was valued then at three million pounds. It consisted of ivory and gold, and diamonds taken from mines at Kimberley by his young warriors.

The story of Lobengula's treasure concealment was told by his half-caste secretary, John Jacobs. Hearing of the approach of the British forces, Lobengula ordered his two large safes and his store of ivory to be loaded onto ox wagons. He and Jacobs set forth, accompanied by four indunas, or headmen, and fourteen tribesmen. From Lobengula's *kraal*, near the modern city of Bulawayo, the expedition went northwards and then eastwards, crossing the Zambezi River before reaching a wild area of bush and jungle.

At this remote spot a great pit was dug. The safes and ivory were placed in it and then covered with rocks before the pit was refilled. Markers were set up. That night Lobengula ordered the indunas to slay the guards as they slept. Only Jacobs and the indunas survived with the secret, for Lobengula died from fever on the banks of the Zambezi.

John Jacobs later went to live in South Africa. He agreed to lead treasure seekers to the spot, but was refused entry into Rhodesia. He revealed his secret to two Germans who searched for the treasure without success. They returned to the German colony in South West Africa, where they filed their story in the archives.

The German colony fell to the South Africans at the start of the 1914–18 War. At that time an English land surveyor called Lytton heard about the strange expedition. He searched the German archives and found papers, written in code, and a map. With the aid of the Germans' map, Lytton narrowed the area of search to thirty square miles at a spot across the Zambezi. This lay in Portuguese territory which is now the modern state of Mozambique.

Lytton travelled to the area in a model T Ford. He located the spot indicated by the markers which Lobengula had left. Digging disclosed the bones of Lobengula's guards. Lytton persuaded his porters to dig deeper, but the trench collapsed, burying ten men.

Lytton planned to make one more attempt to dig up the treasure in 1934. By then his search had become well-known. The Portuguese government were claiming fifty per cent of the treasure and the De Beers Mining Company laid claim to the diamonds, which it alleged had been stolen from its mines. The London Missionary Society, acting as trustee for the Matabele people, also put in a claim for fifty per cent of the treasure.

Lytton abandoned his quest in the face of these legal problems. He returned to the spot, filled in the trench, and replaced the markers, hoping that one day the Matabele might be able to return and claim their inheritance.

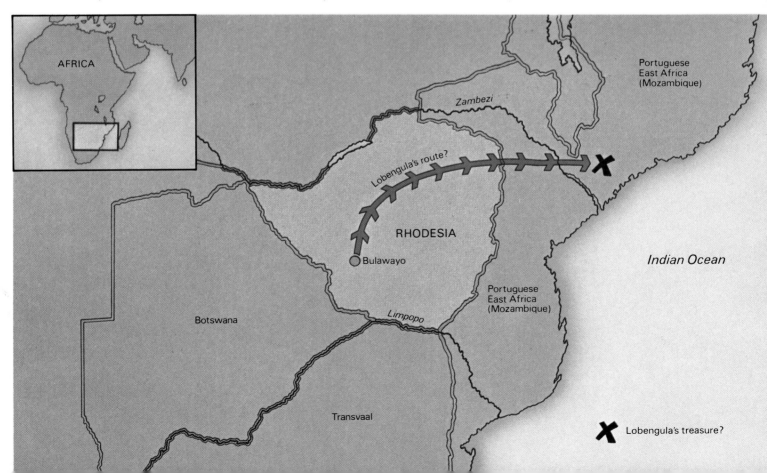

Lobengula's treasure?

The Lost Dutchman Mine

In the Superstition Mountains of Arizona there is said to be a rich goldmine. It is known as the Lost Dutchman Mine and is the great legend of America's southwestern states.

In 1847 a Mexican family called the Peraltas acquired knowledge of the mine. They organized an expedition and returned from the mine laden with gold. Unknown to the Peraltas, the mine lay in sacred Apache territory and on the way back they were massacred by a party of Apaches.

During the 1860s, two Prussian immigrants arrived in the town of Arizpe, Mexico, the home of the Peraltas. They became friendly with a surviving member of the family, Don Miguel, who told them of the mine. Don Miguel and the two men, Waltz and Weiser, journeyed to the mine and returned with gold. Waltz and Weiser shared half of the gold.

Don Miguel gave temporary ownership to the two Prussians in return for a share of their profits. The two men worked the mine, but one day Waltz found his partner dead, spreadeagled over a fire. This gruesome practice was known to be an Apache custom. Waltz worked the mine on his own for some time and on his death its location was lost. Although he was a German, it was Waltz whom the mine was named after.

Another story gives evidence of the existence of the mine. Around 1865 Dr Abraham Thorne gave medical

▶ In 1847 the Peralta family heard about a rich goldmine deep in the Superstition Mountains of Arizona. They mounted a huge expedition and returned from the mine laden with gold. On the journey back to Arizpe they were massacred by a party of Apaches who ambushed them from the rocks above. The Apaches were not interested in their gold and left it where it had fallen on the floor of the canyon. The Peraltas were murdered because they had trespassed on the sacred ground of the Apaches.

▼ A copy of one of the Peralta maps which Adolph Ruth used in his search for the Lost Dutchman Mine. The maps were given to Ruth by his son, who had acquired them from a descendant of the Peraltas in return for saving his life. Adolph Ruth was a keen amateur treasure hunter. He made the mistake of going into the Superstition Mountains alone.

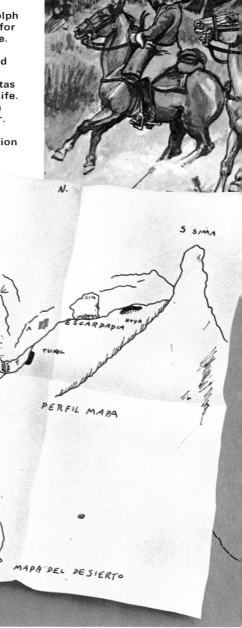

treatment to the Apaches. In return for his help, the Indians rewarded him. He was blindfolded and taken on horseback into the mountains. When the blindfold was removed, Dr Thorne saw that he was in a narrow canyon dominated by a pinnacle of rock. At his feet were piles of gold. The rock has since been identified as Weaver's Needle, a prominent landmark, which modern treasure hunters believe is near the site of the Lost Dutchman Mine. Dr Thorne returned from this remote spot with a gift of gold from the Apaches.

In the 1930s a man called Adolph Ruth acquired a set of maps said to have been drawn by the Peraltas. Armed with the maps, Ruth set off alone into the mountains to search for the mine. He disappeared. Six months later his body was found, the skull pierced by a bullet hole. In his clothing were some notes with the scribbled words 'Veni, vidi, vici', Latin for 'I came, I saw, I conquered'. Did this mean that Ruth had located the Lost Dutchman Mine? Further search revealed that his killer had made off with the maps. Since Ruth's death, there have been many attempts to find the mine, but no one appears to have been successful.

▲ The Superstition Mountains of Arizona lie forty miles from Phoenix. Many treasure seekers have died in attempts to find the Lost Dutchman Mine. Some have died accidentally, or because they were poorly-equipped, but there have also been strange disappearances, shootings and unexplained avalanches of rock.

The Money Pit

Does an immense treasure lie in the depths of the Money Pit? This deep shaft lies on Oak Island, Nova Scotia. Many North Americans believe that great wealth awaits the skilled engineer who can overcome the pit's ingenious defences. Several syndicates and many individuals have spent at least two million dollars in vain endeavour to defeat the genius who dug the pit and harnessed the tides to defend it.

Three boys discovered the pit in 1795 when they visited Oak Island. They found a recently-made clearing among the oak trees. In the centre stood an ancient oak. One of its branches had been lopped off, and under the stump was a depression in the ground. The boys suspected a treasure concealment and dug into the pit. They removed several platforms of oak logs, sealed with putty. At 27 metres (90 ft) their picks struck a hard obstruction, but when they returned to the pit next day, they found it flooded to within 10 metres (33 ft) of ground level. No amount of bailing and pumping could lower the level of the water.

On the beach they found a specially-constructed drain. This was connected to a subterranean tunnel 152 metres long (500 ft), which carried sea water into the pit. The excavators dynamited the tunnel, but the sea continued to flow into the pit. Later it was found that a second flood tunnel ran into the pit at a deeper level. Over time the pit has become a welter of mud. To excavate it now would cost a million dollars, a sum unlikely to be raised because excavators have found no evidence of treasure.

But what was the purpose of the pit, if not to conceal treasure? The construction of the pit and the flood tunnels would have required the knowledge of a skilled engineer and the labour of several miners. Who were these men? Did they return to recover their treasure? If so, they too would have been defeated by the flooding of the pit. The oak platforms made airlocks which had held down the level of the sea. Removal of the oak platforms allowed the sea to surge up, flooding the pit. No one, not even the original constructors, could reach its depths. What then is the answer?

Having excavated the pit, the engineer may have dug upwards and outwards from the shaft and made treasure concealments close to the surface. In this way he would overcome the danger of disturbing the soil, a tell-tale clue that someone had been digging. Having done this, he and his men would have connected the flood tunnels, placed the oak platforms in position, and filled in the pit with earth. Anyone who attempted to excavate the pit would fail. The engineer alone would know the true position of his treasure cache.

Whether further search will reveal treasure on Oak Island is anyone's guess. Even more intriguing is the identity of the genius who devised a defence system which has defied the efforts of modern technology.

▲ A view of Oak Island. In the centre, a group of treasure hunters is at work around the Money Pit. The two flood tunnels run from the Money Pit to Smith's Cove, the bay at the lower right.

▼ A close-up view of excavations at the Money Pit led by George J. Greene, a Texas oilman. His syndicate was prepared to spend money without limit to prove or disprove the legend of Oak Island.

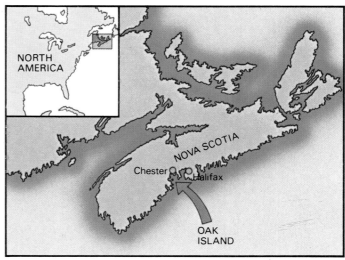

▲ A battle between English troops and American rebels during the American War of Independence. The Money Pit was constructed at the time of this war. One theory suggests that the pit could have been dug by the Royal Engineers, the only people in America at that time capable of carrying out such an operation.

▶ The Money Pit is 4 metres (13 ft) wide and 53 metres (175 ft) deep. The engineers who built it inserted a layer of oak logs sealed with putty at each 3 metre (10 ft) level. They left an obstruction at 27 metres (90 ft), possibly as a decoy, and ran two tunnels to the shore at 33 metres (110 ft) and 45 metres (150 ft). These carried seawater from the beach which flooded the shaft only after the airtight oak platforms had been removed. No one, not even the pit's original designers, could have entered the shaft after it had become flooded. This disposes of the long-held theory that the bottom of the shaft contains a chamber filled with treasure chests. Modern treasure hunters are still trying to excavate the shaft but their task is made difficult now the shaft is waterlogged and filled with mud. No one has been able to trace the direction of the second tunnel, which continues to flood the pit. There is no direct evidence that there is any treasure to be found.

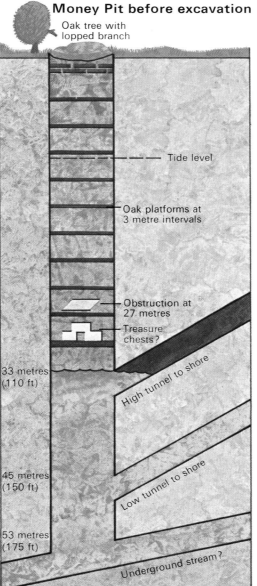

Money Pit before excavation

Oak tree with lopped branch

Tide level

Oak platforms at 3 metre intervals

Obstruction at 27 metres

Treasure chests?

33 metres (110 ft)

High tunnel to shore

45 metres (150 ft)

Low tunnel to shore

53 metres (175 ft)

Underground stream?

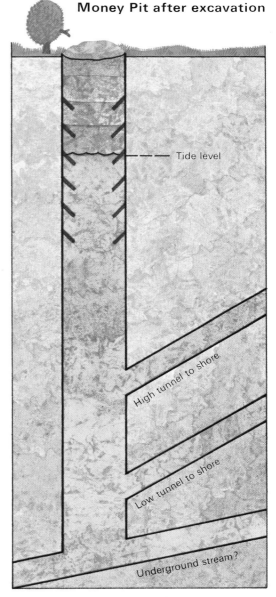

Money Pit after excavation

Tide level

High tunnel to shore

Low tunnel to shore

Underground stream?

A treasure hunter's guide

Thousands of people go treasure hunting. For most of them it is an exciting hobby. They may find a coin or two, or turn up an ancient artefact valuable only to the archaeologist. Others make a business of it, diving for galleon wrecks or tracking down lost gold or silver mines.

Treasure trove stories usually start with the discovery of the proverbial sea-stained chart, from local rumour, or from someone spotting ancient cannon or cannon balls on the sea bed. There are two types of treasure – treasure deliberately concealed, and treasure which has been lost or sunken. How do we go about finding them?

More often than not, it is a matter of chance. We hear or read of some mysterious disappearance of wealth, or of a lost ship, or of some apparently inexplicable soil formation. The first information one hears is nearly always wrong. Tales of treasure become garbled in time until they become wildly exaggerated legends and the 'treasure' progressively increases in value. Beware of those who speak in 'millions'.

The first step in verifying these stories is to trace the earliest records, the best source of information. That is the golden rule of treasure hunting.

Then you must ask yourself 'Did the treasure ever exist?' Or are the stories concerning its concealment or loss no more than romantic legends? The reputed treasure may also have been subsequently recovered. The Spaniards dredged up many ingots from the galleons that sank close to the shores of the Caribbean and adjacent coasts. Checking these facts may require painstaking research in archives and museum libraries.

A world map of treasure sites

This map shows a selection of treasure sites throughout the world. Some of the treasures are well-documented, and many of these have already been salvaged. Others, however, are known only through legends. Their existence may never be proved.

1 The wrecks of several Spanish galleons lie off the western coast of America. The Spaniards sent galleons each year to and from the Philippines, carrying precious commodities.

2 Atahualpa's ransom, 1533. Francisco Pizarro, the Spanish conquistador, held captive the Lord Inca, Atahualpa. In return for the Inca's life, his Indian subjects were to bring vast treasure of gold and silver to the Spaniards. Before all the treasure was received, the Spaniards executed Atahualpa. It is said that the Indians concealed the rest of the treasure in mountain caves and lakes. The treasure has never been found.

3 Since the 1950s, Teddy Tucker has raised treasure from several Spanish galleon wrecks in the Bahamas.

4 Extensive searches have been made in the Caribbean for the wrecks of Spanish treasure galleons lost between the 16th and 18th centuries.

5 In 1830, the *Thetis*, a frigate carrying $810,000 worth of coins and bullion, sank in a gale off the coast of Brazil. The following year British Navy divers, using diving bells, recovered three-quarters of the treasure.

6 The *Laurentic* was torpedoed in 1917 off the coast of Northern Ireland. She carried £5 million in gold bars destined for the United States. After salvage operations 25 gold bars remained in the wreck.

7 Did the Fifth Marquis of Winchester conceal his family's silver and gold in the Old Basing House during the English Civil War? The status of the house as an ancient monument prevents the present owner from excavating for the treasure.

8 The *Lutine* was wrecked off the coast of the Netherlands in 1799. She was a British pay-ship carrying bullion worth £2 million. Little of the treasure has been salvaged owing to dangerous storms and tides. The wreck is now covered in deep layers of silt and sand. The bronze bell of the *Lutine* was one of the few objects to be recovered. It now hangs at Lloyd's, the underwriters, where it is rung whenever a ship is lost.

9 A vast hoard of treasure accumulated by the Nazis is reputed to have been thrown

The best advice is to think first and dig, or dive, later. Far too many over-eager treasure hunters can't wait to begin. The process of learning the true facts leads to another difficulty. Vital clues may be possessed by suspicious people who are afraid to share their knowledge with others who may hold the missing link.

The search for sunken treasure poses other problems. For diving, special equipment is needed. The recent perfection of the aqualung diving gear has made the search for ancient wrecks possible. The location and cargoes of some can be checked at the Archives of the Indies at Seville, Spain, or from other maritime records. They may also show whether any part of the cargo was salvaged soon after the ship went down.

Treasure hunters need to take heed of the law. The law of Treasure Trove varies in each country and searchers should learn how they stand before they dive or dig. They should then obtain a Licence to Search, or report any find at once. It is advisable to learn what percentage of any proceeds must be given up. This can vary from ten to fifty per cent. The government may wish to retain particular articles, in which case it should reward the finder by agreed valuation.

'Treasure Trove' means articles of silver and gold which have been concealed with intention of recovery and of which no owner can be traced. Articles placed in graves, which were not buried with intention of recovery (as at Sutton Hoo), belong to the owner of the land. Lost treasures such as shipwrecked cargoes usually belong to the country in whose territorial waters the ships were lost. But in some cases the original owners or their insurers may retain ownership.

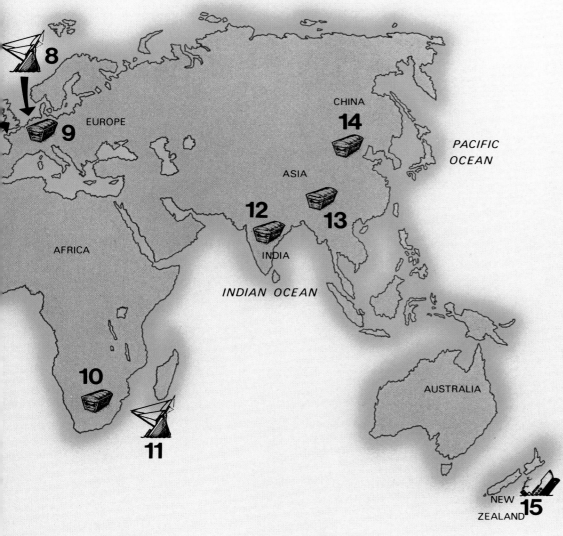

into an Austrian lake at the end of the Second World War.

10 President Kruger is said to have buried a fortune in gold bars somewhere in the Transvaal at the end of the Boer War (1900).

11 In 1783 the British East Indiaman, the *Grosvenor* was wrecked on the coast of South Africa. She was carrying a cargo of gold and jewels worth £300,000. Attempts to salvage the wreck have been largely unsuccessful.

12 Vast treasures of the Indian princes are reputed to have been concealed when India gained independence in 1947.

13 The priceless tomb of Genghis Khan, the Mongol warrior, is said to await discovery in the Gobi Desert.

14 Chinese archaeologists recently found the jade-covered effigy of a princess in a tomb near Peking.

15 The *Niagara*, carrying gold from Australia to Canada, was sunk by a German mine off the eastern coast of New Zealand in 1940. In 1941, 94 per cent of the gold was salvaged but 45 ingots of gold worth £150,000 remain in or near the wreck.

Treasure hunting techniques

Treasure hunting often requires the use of special techniques and equipment. Divers in search of sunken treasure need apparatus to enable them to breathe and avoid the danger of compression disease, often known as the 'bends'.

The first diving equipment invented was the diving bell, which often consisted of no more than an upturned bucket or cask. This could only be used for shallow dives because the air would be used up quickly. In deep water a diver has difficulty expanding his lungs because of the water pressure on his chest. Reinforced steel diving suits were invented to shield the diver from this pressure. These suits were designed with flexible joints so that the diver could work with his hands. When the Sorima Company were salvaging the *Egypt* they found that the simple observation shell equipped with a telephone was the most efficient equipment.

A real revolution came in 1934, when Jacques Yves Cousteau perfected the aqualung equipment. The diver, clad in a rubber suit, face mask and flippers, carried his own cylinder of air. He could move about at will as long as the air lasted. But as in the case of the conventional suit, aqualung diving has its limitations.

In particular the diver faces the danger of compression disease from staying too long at critical depths or ascending to the surface too quickly. Air is made up of oxygen and nitrogen. When a diver breathes under pressure, nitrogen is forced into his tissues. When the diver surfaces and begins to breathe at normal air pressure, the nitrogen expands and tries to force its way out of the tissues. This is compression disease, or the 'bends'. It causes great pain in the diver's joints and muscles. If the pressure is released slowly, the diver's body can release the nitrogen gradually, and the danger of 'bends' is avoided. This can be done in two ways. The diver can surface slowly, with a long wait at each stage, or he can surface quickly and spend a period inside a decompression chamber.

Above right: Salvage operations in 1750. Diving bells have been used for centuries to give divers a supply of air.

From left to right: Diving suits of 1827 and 1855, and a reinforced steel suit with movable joints. In 1837, August Siebe invented an armoured suit in which the diver was supplied with air pumped down from a ship. This restricted his movements and there was danger that the air-link could be snapped or become tangled in wreckage or rocks.

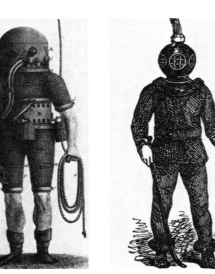

▼ A diver discovers ancient coins from a wreck off the Shetland Islands. Modern divers have a vast array of equipment to aid them in the search for sunken treasure. This diver is using an air-lift pipe which sucks up sand to reveal the treasure beneath.

▶ Modern divers wearing aqualung equipment off the coast of Turkey. The baskets contain salvaged artefacts from a Roman wreck. These divers have their own submerged decompression chamber, which one of the divers has just entered.

Metal detectors

A metal detector in use. This equipment indicates the presence of iron on land and beneath the sea. There may be as many as 200 types on the market. They range from simple models used for finding lost objects, to sophisticated machines which require great skill to operate. A simple detector may locate a pin at a few inches or a cannon ball at ten feet. Their range is strictly limited. They work by means of an electronic pulse which reflects off the object and gives a ping or boom sound.

How to find out more

There is no easy answer to the question 'Where do I go to find out more?' Each treasure story requires research at some particular place. For example, to find out about lost Spanish treasure galleons one must always contact the Archives of the Indies at Seville in Spain.

The best source of information may be the library or museum nearest to the site you are investigating. Unfortunately much useful information may be in private hands and therefore difficult to trace. Much published material, particularly general books about treasure stories, can be incorrect and misleading. The best books to read are those written by the people who were actually involved.

History Comes Alive

Christiane Desroches-Noblecourt: *Tutankhamen*, The Connoisseur and Michael Joseph, 1963
Leonard Cottrell: *The Secrets of Tutankhamen*, Evans Brothers, 1965
British Museum: *Treasures of Tutankhamun*, 1972
John Allegro: *The Treasures of the Copper Scroll*, Routledge & Kegan Paul, 1960
Pearson & Connor: *The Dorak Affair*, Michael Joseph, 1967
Rupert Bruce-Mitford: *The Sutton Hoo Ship Burial: A Handbook*, British Museum, 1972
Magnus Magnusson: *Introducing Archaeology*, The Bodley Head, 1972

Treasure from the Sea

Kip Wagner/L.B. Taylor Jr: *Pieces of Eight*, Longmans, 1967
Latil and Rivoire: *Sunken Treasure*, Rupert Hart-Davis, 1962
Paul Johnstone: *The Archaeology of Ships*, The Bodley Head, 1974
David Scott: *Seventy Fathoms Deep*, Faber & Faber, 1931, (the *Egypt*)
Roger Hart: *Battle of the Spanish Armada*, Wayland, 1973
George F. Bass: *A History of Seafaring*, Thames and Hudson, 1972
Robert Stenuit: *Treasures of the Armada*, David & Charles, 1972
Roland Morris: *Island Treasure*, Hutchinson, 1969 (the *Association*)

Legendary Treasures

Curt Gentry: *The Killer Mountains*, André Deutsch, 1971 (the Lost Dutchman Mine)
Rupert Furneaux: *The Money Pit Mystery*, Tom Stacey, 1972
David Mitchell: *Pirates*, Thames and Hudson, 1976

General

Rupert Furneaux: *The Great Treasure Hunts*, Odhams, 1969
Karl Meyer: *The Plundered Past: The Traffic in Art Treasures*, Hamish Hamilton, 1974

Rules for treasure hunters

1 Investigate fully the stories you hear. Many are based on oft-repeated tales which have become garbled or 'improved' in the telling. Go back to the earliest sources of information. That is the golden rule of treasure hunting.

2 Ask yourself whether the treasure ever really existed. If so, has it been salvaged or found already?

3 Obtain accurate maps or charts. If place names are mentioned which no longer exist, geographical features may help to identify them.

4 Visit and survey your site. Ask questions locally. You will probably learn more by being truthful than by secrecy.

5 Do not dig or dive until you have discovered the legal position. Always obtain permission or a licence to search.

6 Do not make random searches, especially with electronic devices. You may destroy valuable archaeological evidence.

7 Keep exact records of your surveys and work. You may need to refer back to earlier excavations.

8 Don't be too optimistic. Few treasure hunters succeed. But you may have a lot of fun trying.

9 Think first and dig later.

Index